Lust

SAGE SERIES ON CLOSE RELATIONSHIPS

Series Editors
Clyde Hendrick, Ph.D., and
Susan S. Hendrick, Ph.D.

In this series...

ROMANTIC LOVE
by Susan S. Hendrick and Clyde Hendrick

COURTSHIP
by Rodney M. Cate and Sally A. Lloyd

ADULT FRIENDSHIP
by Rosemary Blieszner and Rebecca G. Adams

TWO CAREERS/ONE FAMILY
by Lucia Albino Gilbert

SELF-DISCLOSURE
by Valerian J. Derlega, Sandra Metts,
Sandra Petronio, and Stephen T. Margulis

SEXUALITY
by Susan Sprecher and Kathleen McKinney

FACEWORK
by William R. Cupach and Sandra Metts

MEANINGFUL RELATIONSHIPS
by Steve Duck

REMARRIED FAMILY RELATIONSHIPS
by Lawrence H. Ganong and Marilyn Coleman

RELATIONSHIP CONFLICT
by Daniel J. Canary, William R. Cupach, and Susan J. Messman

RELATIONSHIPS IN CHRONIC ILLNESS AND DISABILITY
by Renee F. Lyons, Michael J. L. Sullivan, and Paul G. Ritvo
with James C. Coyne

FRIENDSHIP PROCESSES
by Beverley Fehr

SOCIAL SUPPORT IN COUPLES
by Carolyn E. Cutrona

ADULT ATTACHMENT
by Judith Feeney and Patricia Noller

GENDER AND CLOSE RELATIONSHIPS
by Barbara A. Winstead, Valarian J. Derlega, and Suzanna Rose

MARITAL EQUALITY
by Janice M. Steil

LUST
by Pamela C. Regan and Ellen Berscheid

Lust

What We Know About
Human Sexual Desire

Pamela C. Regan
Ellen Berscheid

Sage
Series
on Close
Relationships

Sage Publications, Inc.
International Educational and Professional Publisher
Thousand Oaks ■ London ■ New Delhi

For information:

Sage Publications, Inc.
2455 Teller Road
Thousand Oaks, California 91320
E-mail: order@sagepub.com

Sage Publications Ltd.
6 Bonhill Street
London EC2A 4PU
United Kingdom

Sage Publications India Pvt. Ltd.
M-32 Market
Greater Kailash I
New Delhi 110 048 India

Printed in the United States of America

Library of Congress Cataloging-in-Publication Data

Main entry under title:

Regan, Pamela C.
    Lust : What we know about human sexual desire / by Pamela C.
Regan and Ellen Berscheid.
        p. cm. — (Sage series on close relationships)
    Includes bibliographical references.
    ISBN 0-7619-1792-6 (alk. paper)
    ISBN 0-7619-1793-4 (alk. paper)
    1. Sex. 2. Desire. 3. Lust. I. Berscheid, Ellen. II. Title. III.
Series.
    HQ21 .R3 1999
    306.7—dc21   99-6175

99 00 01 02 03 04 9 8 7 6 5 4 3 2 1

Acquiring Editor: C. Terry Hendrix/Jim Brace-Thompson
Typesetter/Designer: Danielle Dillahunt

Contents

Preface   vii

1. Sexual Desire: Historical Perspectives   1

2. Sexual Desire: The Phenomenon   12

3. Sexual Desire: The Body (Part I)   32

4. Sexual Desire: The Body (Part II)   53

5. Sexual Desire: The Mind   69

6. Sexual Desire: The Partner and the Relationship   88

7. Sexual Desire and Romantic Love   110

8. Sexual Desire: Future Directions   137

References   141

Index   169

About the Authors   173

Preface

"What Makes a Woman Bedable?" (*Cosmopolitan*)

"60 Wild, Erotic Ways to Excite Your Lover" (*Woman's Own*)

"Love vs. Lust: How You'll Know the Difference" (*Woman's Own*)

"How to Spark His Desire (Again & Again & Again)" (*Redbook*)

"Guy Expectations: How to Get What You Want" (*Teen*)

"Sex Made Easy" (*Men's Health*)

"Hot, Fast Sex: The Quick and the Bed" (*Men's Fitness*)

"Supercharged Sex: How to Find a Like-Minded Partner" (*Exercise & Health*)

"Sex-cess! Get Lucky . . . Tonight!" (*Exercise & Health*)

"What Women Really Want" (*Men's Fitness*)

These quotations, taken from the headlines of several contemporary men's and women's magazines, underscore the almost obsessive fascination with which the media and the reading public approach the topic of sexual desire. Popular music, television, and film provide countless depictions of sexually passionate relationships, alternately glorifying and vilifying the desires of the flesh. On a daily basis, talk show hosts and their invited guests tell us how to behave in a sexually desirable manner, what to say to communicate sexual desire to an attractive other, and what clothes to wear to ignite sexual desire in our current flames. Should this advice fail, we can always turn to the countless self-help books that promise to teach us in 10 easy steps how to rekindle the sexual ashes of our fading romances, once-torrid love affairs, or weatherbeaten marriages. All of these events conspire to teach us that sexual desire is a necessary ingredient in our romantic relationships and that sexual desirability is something we each should strive to attain.

That sexual desire is associated with and has implications for several meaningful experiences in human life will come as no surprise to our readers. What will come as a surprise, perhaps, is the fact that sexual desire has only recently emerged as a topic considered worthy of rigorous scientific investigation. As a result, although as private citizens we may think a lot (and think we know a lot) about sexual desire, there is a dearth of research and theory on this topic in the professional literature. In addition, what little information there is can be found buried here and there within a variety of disciplines, including biology and medicine, psychology and philosophy, sex and marital therapy, sociology and anthropology, and ethology (to name a few). Because traditionally there has been very little communication among these disciplines, the interested student of this aspect of human experience finds himself or herself faced with an unorganized mishmash of contradictory theoretical statements and confusing empirical data.

Our goal in writing this monograph is to dispel some of this confusion by reviewing and bringing together in one volume past and present theory, supposition, and knowledge about sexual desire. Although we write primarily from a social psychological perspective, our general approach is interdisciplinary in that we incorporate material from a multitude of fields. The eight chapters encompass a wide range of theoretical and empirical work. Chapter 1 sets the stage by considering the study of sexual desire from a historical perspective. In particular, we discuss how the emphasis placed by early sex researchers on abnormal sexuality, on animal sexuality, and on overt physiological and behavioral sexual responses contributed to the neglect of such subjective, psychological sexual phenomena such as sexual desire. We then review work in clinical and social psychology that led to the emergence of sexual desire as a topic worthy of scientific scrutiny.

Of course, any discussion of sexual desire must first specify the characteristic manifestations of this experience. Thus, Chapter 2 focuses on the phenomenon of sexual desire—what it is and what events serve to indicate its occurrence. We describe characteristics of a state of (general) desire, distinguish sexual desire from both sexual arousal and sexual activity, and present the various theoretical approaches to sexual desire and its measurement.

We are particularly interested in reviewing research pertinent to the causal dynamics of sexual desire. Chapters 3 and 4 consider the "body" of desire—that is, all the hormonal, biological, and physical factors that contribute to and influence the experience of sexual desire. We examine how people's feelings of sexual desire are related to hormone levels and hormonally mediated life events (e.g., menstruation), chronological age, biological sex, physical health, and drug use.

In Chapter 5, we turn from the physical to the mental. In particular, we explore how social norms, affective expectancies, previous experiences, personality variables, mood, and emotional state may contribute to the experience of sexual desire. Because what people believe about sexual desire may influence their behavior, we also present data from our own descriptive research on men's and women's beliefs about the nature and causes of sexual desire.

Emotions, expectancies, and beliefs often are experienced about and within a specific relationship with a particular partner. Chapter 6 considers various partner characteristics that may incite sexual desire, including physical attractiveness, physique and physique display, social status and dominance, novelty, and pheromones. In addition, we review research on the association between sexual desire and relational events (e.g., communication, satisfaction, adjustment).

Chapter 7 continues our exploration of the interpersonal aspects of sexual desire by focusing on the relationship between sexual desire and passionate love. The first part of this chapter examines theoretical statements about the link, if any, between these two experiences; the second reviews indirect and direct empirical evidence that speaks to this question.

We conclude, in Chapter 8, by considering the personal, interpersonal, and societal implications of sexual desire—the experience itself, as well as beliefs about its nature, causes, and meaning.

Sexual desire plays an important role in human lives and human interpersonal relationships. We hope that this book sheds some small degree of light on this fascinating and understudied topic.

‌ Acknowledgments

We gratefully acknowledge the assistance of several individuals who contributed in various ways to this work. In particular, we would like to thank Susan and Clyde Hendrick for their initial interest in and their sustained commitment to this project; C. Terry Hendrix for believing that a book on sexual desire would make an important contribution to the literature and to the **Sage Series on Close Relationships**; David Soltz (Dean, School of Natural and Social Sciences) and Michael Roffe (Chairperson, Department of Psychology) of California State University, Los Angeles for providing the first author with leave time to complete this work; and our friends, colleagues, and family (human and nonhuman) for their guidance, support, and encouragement during the tenure of this project.

1

Sexual Desire
Historical Perspectives

In this increasingly liberal political and social climate, courses on human sexuality and "sex education" appear with regularity in college, high school, and even junior high school curricula. Consequently, sexuality textbooks now abound, and it is to one of these texts that the student interested in sexual desire is likely to go to learn more about the subject. Unfortunately, what the student finds in human sexuality texts is an almost exclusive focus on the physiology of sexual response. There are wonderfully exact depictions of human sexual anatomy, volumes of information about the prevalence of various sexual behaviors, and detailed lists of the genital and physiological events associated with sexual arousal. But there is very little mention of sexual desire, the essential spark that ignites the human sexual apparatus that is so precisely detailed. When, and if, sexual desire is mentioned, it is primarily in discussions of sexual disorders or problems. Why is sexual desire, the center of the whole sexual show, sitting on the sidelines in human sexuality texts? The answer is that there simply isn't much known about it. And there isn't much known about it because early sex research focused on abnormal or pathological sexual phenomena, on animal sexuality, and on physiological, behavioral sexual events. In this chapter, we discuss how these historical events contributed to a neglect of sexual desire and then we consider the factors that led to the emergence of sexual desire as a topic of scientific investigation.

❧ Early Sex Research

For many hundreds of years, the "scientific" study of the origins and manifestations of various aspects of human sexuality was the province of a handful of physicians and clerics who wrote their treatises primarily for each other rather than for the general public. These men (and they were exclusively men) focused almost entirely on sexual behavior they viewed as abnormal, gleaning their "facts" and drawing their conclusions from religious theology, criminal records, medical case studies, clandestine visits to local mental wards, and hearsay.

Masturbation, for example, was one such abnormal behavior that captured their attention. In *Three Hundred Years of Psychiatry*, Hunter and MacAlpine (1963) state that masturbation became firmly established as a primary cause of mental illness and nervous disorders in the minds of professionals and nonprofessionals alike by the 19th century. According to these historians, the English clergyman Richard Baxter (1615-1691) spent a great deal of his time and energy gravely warning his flock against the evils of masturbation. Similarly, the anonymous 18th-century treatise, titled *Onania: Or, the Heinous Sin of Self-Pollution*, listed gonorrhea, impotence, erectile dysfunction, barrenness, epilepsy, consumption, loss of limbs, sleep disorders, and general pain among the ills caused by the "impure" practice. To those dire consequences of masturbation, the Swiss physician Simon André Tissot (1728-1797) was to add degeneration of the spine, blindness, and brain disease.

The exclusive focus on the mental and physical problems associated with sexual behavior that dominated early medical and religious discourses created an environment in which the sexual aspect of human experience became characterized as a wicked siren waiting to drag weak persons into Hell or push them over the edge into insanity. For example, the glimpse of human sexuality provided in the pages of German physician Richard von Krafft-Ebing's (1886/1945) masterpiece *Psychopathia Sexualis* is replete with "abominable and nauseating" (p. 497) sexual acts perpetrated by a motley assortment of masturbators, rapists, pedophiles, sadists, masochists, transvestites, necrophiliacs, fetishists, voyeurs, frotteurs, and other disturbed individuals. Krafft-Ebing (1840-1902), in fact, wrote his treatise in an attempt to inform legislation and jurisprudence about the nature of certain sexual aberrations. His work, which contained hundreds of graphically detailed case histories garnered from the consulting room, mental clinics, and law courts, was not created as a handbook for public consumption. To the contrary, its scientific title, obtuse medical terminology, and Latin-riddled text represented a deliberate (but ultimately unsuccessful) attempt to discourage the general public from reading information reserved for Krafft-Ebing's legal, medical, and forensic colleagues. In the preface to the 12th edition, for example, he voices his thanks for the favorable criticism accorded previous editions in "professional circles" (p. iii) and states that he has increased the number of technical terms and made freer use of the Latin language as well.

The English physician Havelock Ellis (1859-1939), the central figure in the emergence of the modern study of human sexuality, was a product of this pathologically oriented and secretive climate. His monumental, seven-volume work, *Studies in the Psychology of Sex* (1897-1928), was the first of its kind written to inform the general public as well as the scientific community. In the Foreword to the 1938 printing of a condensed version of the manual, in fact, Ellis thanks both medical *and* laypersons for their cordial reception of previous editions. Unlike his predecessors, Ellis focused primarily on non-pathological sexual phenomena and attempted to explain sexual behavior in both men and women as a normal aspect of human development and function. For example, he viewed the prevalence of homosexual behavior among animals, early human societies, and modern men as evidence that homosexuality should be classified as an anomaly rather than as a degeneration or disease. Moreover, he argued forcefully that masturbation was so widespread a human behavior that it could no longer be viewed as "abnormal." This was the first time, too, that an attempt was made to determine the influence of social forces on individual sexuality. Ellis believed that the high incidence of "frigidity" found in many 19th-century women was not in most cases the result of some naturally occurring biological deficit in the sexual impulse but, rather, the combined result of their partners' inadequate sexual skills, of societal and religious mores, of ignorance of sexual matters and poor education in general, and of the late age at which intercourse typically first occurred (e.g., Ellis, 1933/1963).

Like his contemporary Havelock Ellis, Sigmund Freud (1856-1939) also emphasized sex as a central aspect of normal human development, constructing an elaborate psychoanalytic theory that conceived of the sexual instinct, or *libido*, as the primary motivating force of all human behavior. Freud scandalized his peers by suggesting that children, formerly viewed as innocent, sexless beings not yet subject to the raging hormonal influences of adolescence and adulthood, were in fact brought into the world with their sexual instincts and propensities for sexual activities wholly intact. Indeed, Freud argued vociferously that the autoerotic behaviors or genital reactions sometimes seen in infants were not the simple reflexes they were assumed to be at the time but were in fact physical manifestations of a very necessary sexual impulse that would pass through a series of stages and eventually develop into the normal sexuality of the adult (e.g., Freud, 1905/1938, 1910/1977).

In short, the almost exclusive focus on "abnormal" or "diseased" sexual behavior that pervaded the work of early sex researchers promulgated the notion that human sexuality was a mysterious and awesome beast whose systematic inspection at close range was best left to trained professionals. Interestingly, even Freud and Ellis, who labored so feverishly to bring sex out of the mental wards and prisons and into polite society, were not immune to the influence of the clannish and pathologically oriented climate that characterized earlier research. Like their predecessors Tissot, Rush, and Krafft-Ebing, Freud and Ellis derived most of their knowledge of sexual phenomena from systematic observations of what social psychologist Donn Byrne, in his 1977 review of social psychology and the study of sexual behavior, ruefully referred to as "animal sex, native sex, and crazy sex" (p. 4). Freud, for example, based much of his theory on knowledge gained from his own personal experience of psychoanalysis as well as from the analyses of a relatively small number of disturbed patients; Ellis relied on case histories collected from colleagues, correspondents, and friends, as well as on data garnered from medical archives. Thus, although by the early 20th century, scientists interested in human sexuality were beginning to make tentative steps toward open discourse about questions of sexuality, they continued to restrict themselves to an examination of clinical populations and to "abnormal" aspects of human sexual experience.

❧ Alfred Kinsey and the Modern Study of Human Sexual Behavior

This state of affairs began to change in the mid-20th century, when a few courageous individuals began to break the unspoken rules that had guided much of the earlier work on human sexuality and to conduct empirical research on the sexual behaviors and attitudes of the ordinary person. However, the first of these modern sex researchers tended to focus primarily on discrete behavioral, physical, or physiological events that could be readily observed and tabulated, while ignoring, or deeming unimportant, more intangible, subjective aspects of sexuality (such as sexual desire).

For example, Alfred Kinsey (1894-1956) and his colleagues Wardell Pomeroy, Clyde Martin, and Paul Gebhard were the first to quantify the study of human sexuality. Kinsey, a biology professor at Indiana University in the mid-1930s, was confronted with the daunting task of designing and teaching a marriage and family course in the summer of 1938. To his dismay, he found that little scientifically valid information was available about the sexual aspects of marriage. In response, he and his group began a program of research designed to fill the missing gaps in the literature. At first, this endeavor took the form of questionnaires that asked about the sexual experiences and histories of the students in Kinsey's classes. By the end of 1938, however, the Kinsey research team had graduated to conducting face-to-face, individual interviews using a standardized questionnaire, and they had broadened their subject population to include the American public. Data from approximately 12,000 interviews gathered over a decade were incorporated into two works, *Sexual Behavior in the Human Male* (Kinsey, Pomeroy, & Martin, 1948) and *Sexual Behavior in the Human Female* (Kinsey, Pomeroy, Martin, & Gebhard, 1953).

The publication of these compilations of statistics about human sexual behavior met with disbelief and anger from many quarters. Several attempts were made to prevent the publication of the research results and to dismiss Kinsey from his academic post at Indiana University, and the entire group faced opposition at the hands of the police, the legal and medical communities, and many scientific colleagues. That these two books were published during the McCarthy era, a time of intense political repression, no doubt contributed to such harassment. No one had ever dared to openly discuss "unpleasant" topics such as adultery, homosexuality, masturbation, bestiality, and premarital intercourse and, worse, provide statistical evidence that many Americans did such things more frequently than anyone had ever imagined. Indeed, the researchers noted in their 1948 publication that several well-meaning colleagues had suggested that the investigation be confined to "normal" sexual behavior (p. 12). Despite the outcry, however, Kinsey and his colleagues persevered in their efforts, and in so doing, they paved the way for subsequent investigations of sexual behavior and attitudes.

ﻬ   Animal Sexuality: Extrapolating
     From the Barn to the Bedroom

During the period in which Kinsey and colleagues published their data on human sexual behavior, several other researchers interested in human sexuality were examining animal sexual responses. Comparative psychology was at that time a strong subdiscipline within psychology, and it was assumed that researchers could learn about human sexuality by observing the mating behaviors of lower-order mammals and infrahuman primates and then extrapolating from these to humans. In addition, given the kind of outcry that met

Kinsey's research, it was no doubt politically "safer" to study sex in the barn than sex in the bedroom.

Research on animal sexuality focuses on hormones, anatomy, and molar sexual behavior (e.g., Beach, 1976; Ford & Beach, 1951), and researchers of human sexuality have borrowed this biologically and behaviorally based template in their attempts to uncover the mechanisms and correlates of human sexual responses. For example, a vast literature on the hormonal correlates of sexual behavior and arousal in men and women has been established and flourishes, and researchers continue to investigate the relation between sexual activity and hormonally mediated female life events such as menstruation, pregnancy and lactation, and menopause. Extensive efforts also have been made to delineate the effects of the administration of exogenous hormones on the sexual behavior and function of individuals with hormonal abnormalities as well as on the sexual function of sex offenders. In addition, interest in the influence of pheromones on human sexual behavior has increased in recent years, perhaps fueled by the finding that compounds that have pheromonal properties in other animals can be found in the urine and sweat of humans.

Investigation of the influence of hormones and pheromones on sexual behavior is necessary (and we review this research in Chapters 3 and 6). Like our animal cousins, we humans are born with a sexual apparatus that can be coaxed into a state of arousal through the aid of manual manipulation, appropriate levels of circulating hormones, and exposure to erotic stimuli such as the genitals of a sexually receptive partner. These similarities aside, however, sexual phenomena are far more complex in humans than in other animals, as the presence of a more highly developed cerebral cortex in humans would suggest. For example, Reiss (e.g., 1986b) proposes that sexual interaction is important to humans not only because it yields pleasure, but because it allows an individual to disclose (sexually) intimate aspects of the self to others, which in turn may lead to emotional, intellectual, or affectionate disclosure; that is, sexual interaction in humans always possesses an inherent relationship potential. In addition, unlike animals, humans can arouse themselves in the absence of direct stimulation or external erotic stimuli through the use of sexual fantasy—a self-initiated, creative mental process that represents a spontaneous, improvisational, psychological phenomenon not included in the animal sexual response repertoire. Similarly, genital stimulation and exposure to erotic stimuli not only trigger physiological and genital arousal in humans but also can evoke affective, informational, and imaginative responses that in turn mediate sexual arousal (e.g., Byrne, 1977, 1983a, 1983b; Fisher, Byrne, White, & Kelley, 1988).

In conclusion, although certain parallels exist between animal and human sexuality (e.g., we share some of the triggering mechanisms for sexual arousal, and sexual behavior can serve a reproductive purpose), we cannot easily apply what we know of animal sexuality to the human sexual experience. The greater cognitive capacity of humans and the resultant increased role played by psychological phenomena, the multitude of meanings that society places on sexual events and interactions, and the consequences such events and interactions have for the individual all have contributed to vast differences between the two.

✍ Masters and Johnson and the Physiology of Human Sexuality

Like Kinsey and the sex researchers who used templates of animal sexuality to understand human sexual response, William Masters and Virginia Johnson also focused on the physiological and behavioral aspects of sexuality. Challenging scientific and public opinion even more than did Kinsey, these researchers recorded the physiological and genital responses of men and women as they engaged in a variety of sexual behaviors in the laboratory. Masters, an obstetrician-gynecologist at the Washington University School of Medicine, began his work in the field of human sexuality in 1953, just after the second Kinsey book was published. Believing that an understanding of human sexuality must begin with detailed knowledge of sexual anatomy and physiology, this enterprising physician established a laboratory in 1954 in which he and his colleague Virginia Johnson observed and recorded the physical details of what came to be known as the "human sexual response cycle"—a cycle consisting of physiological reactions or processes labeled *excitement, plateau, orgasm,* and *resolution.*

Like Kinsey's behavioral data, this four-phase cycle is noticeably reticent on the topic of sexual desire. Masters and Johnson (1966) simply say this:

> The first or excitement phase of the human cycle of sexual response develops from any source of somatogenic or psychogenic stimulation. The stimulative factor is of major import in establishing sufficient increment of sexual tension to extend the cycle. (p. 5)

They do not elaborate. Rather, the discussion for the excitement phase—as well as discussion of the plateau, orgasm, and resolution phases—focuses on physical responses to increases and decreases in sexual tension, including changes in heart rate, blood flow, muscle tension, breathing patterns, and reproductive organs (e.g., nipple and penis erection, breast and clitoral enlargement, lubrication and lengthening of the vagina). In fact, the only subjective, psychological responses mentioned by Masters and Johnson are those associated with orgasm in men and women. They note, for example, that female orgasm is accompanied or followed by "intense sensual awareness" and a sensation of "suffusion of warmth" (pp. 135-136), and that male orgasm is preceded by a "sensation of ejaculatory inevitability" and subjective "appreciation of fluid volume" (p. 215).

? wtf

❧ The Emergence of Sexual Desire as a Scientific Question

The work of Kinsey and his colleagues and of Masters and Johnson was instrumental in demonstrating that sexuality is a normal part of the human experience as well as an appropriate topic of scientific investigation.[1,2] Both—perhaps necessarily, given the primary focus of their investigations—made only cursory mentions of sexual desire.[3] However, there is more to the human sexual experience than physiological, genital, and behavioral responses. People do not suddenly find themselves flushed, panting, lubricated, tensed, and ready for sexual action; something opens the gates of the sexual response cycle. But what creates the sexual tension and provides impetus to the excitement phase?

Helen Singer Kaplan was one of the first to attempt to answer that question. Discovering that the presenting problem of many of her clients was a lack of interest in sexual activity, this noted clinician and sex therapist argued for the importance of expanding the human sexual response cycle to include a sexual desire phase. In her landmark book, *Disorders of Sexual Desire* (1979), she proposed a triphasic model of human sexuality consisting of three physiologically related but discrete phases: *desire, excitement,* and *orgasm.* Kaplan's vasodilatory excitement phase encompassed Masters and Johnson's excitement and plateau phases, and her orgasm phase directly corresponded to Masters and Johnson's orgasm phase. The initial desire phase was new.

Kaplan's focus was clinical. Her major purpose in distinguishing between the desire phase and the genital phases of excitement and orgasm was to enable clinicians to more effectively target and treat the various dysfunctions associated with each phase. As a result, Kaplan's work contains an impressive discussion of the psychological and physiological factors associated with sexual desire disorders, particularly inhibited or hypoactive sexual desire, which she loosely defines as a loss of interest in sexual matters that is troublesome to the client or the client's partner, as well as a wide array of case studies to illustrate her points and therapeutic techniques. In addition, however, Kaplan added sexual desire to the human sexual response cycle, thereby bringing the concept to the attention of nonclinical researchers and inviting them to acknowledge the importance of subjective aspects of sexuality in their work.

And they have. For example, social psychologists increasingly include sexual desire in their theories of romantic love; evolutionary psychologists have begun to delineate the adaptive functions of desire (e.g., promotion of intercourse and reproduction); communication and emotion theorists have started to explore the communicative potential of expressions of sexual desire; and social constructionists are now considering the manner in which the experience and expression of sexual desire are determined by socialization and learning processes.

This growing recognition that sexual desire has important individual, interpersonal, societal, and even evolutionary implications has created an intense need to examine and understand this aspect of sexuality. It is difficult, however, to study a phenomenon until one knows precisely what is to be studied. In the next chapter, then, we examine theory and research on the phenomenon of sexual desire— what it is, how it differs from other aspects of sexuality, and how it is measured.

❧ Notes

1. That the study of human sexuality is flourishing today can be seen by simply examining the scientific literature. Currently, journals dealing exclusively with sexual and reproductive issues include the *American Journal of Obstetrics and Gynecology, Archives of Sexual Behavior,* the *Canadian Journal of Human Sexuality, Journal of Homosexuality, Journal of Psychology & Human Sexuality, Journal of Sex & Marital Therapy, Journal of Reproduction and Fertility, Medical Aspects of Human Sexuality, Sex Roles, Sexual and Marital Therapy,* and the *Journal of Sex Research.* Sex research also regularly finds expression in "mainstream" psychological outlets such as *Basic and Applied Social Psychology, Journal of Applied Social Psychology, Journal of Personality and Social Psychology, Journal of Research in Personality, Personality and Social Psychology Bulletin, Psychological Bulletin,* and *Social Psychology Quarterly,* as well as in journals devoted to relationship phenomena (i.e., *Journal of Social and Personal Relationships, Personal Relationships*).

2. Unfortunately, the future of sex research is still not ensured. During the early 1990s, Congress and the administration voted to delete the funding originally allocated to a national survey of adult sexual behavior (Youngstrom, 1991). In addition, the Department of Health and Human Services canceled a survey designed to gather data about various kinds of adolescent sexual behaviors, including those that put teens at risk for pregnancy and sexually transmitted diseases, on the grounds that some of the items were too invasive and explicit. Perhaps more frightening, Representative William Dannemeyer introduced an (unadopted) amendment in 1991 during a House debate on a bill reauthorizing the National Institutes of Health that denied federal funding for research on adolescent sexual behavior. Thus, although sex research has come a long way since the time of Krafft-Ebing, Freud, and Havelock Ellis, it is obvious that researchers interested in human sexuality will continue to face disapproval from some segments of the public and will find themselves fighting for funding for their research.

3. These researchers appear to have modified their view somewhat in recent years. Although their focus remains behavioral and physiological, Masters, Johnson, and Kolodny (1994) state in a recent work that "it is certainly true that sexual desire serves as a springboard for subsequent sexual arousal. . . . Because of this, it is useful to view sexual desire as the first phase of the human sexual response cycle, as has been suggested by psychiatrist Helen Singer Kaplan" (p. 46).

2

Sexual Desire

The Phenomenon

Sexual desire is the wanting or the wishing or the urge to have sex or intercourse with a partner or partners. It does not imply that it is the act of sex but it is just the thoughts and emotions going on in one's head when thinking about sex with a person of the opposite sex. It is natural and happens often when around others at a social gathering or wherever. I call it being "horny." [male, age 26]

The young man who provided this statement, a participant in one of our studies (Regan & Berscheid, 1996), clearly views sexual desire as a psychological, subjective state of wanting or wishing for sex. It is equally clear from his response that he considers sexual desire to be separate from sexual behavior or activity. Is he correct in these assumptions? Most of us would probably think so. In fact, we began this work under the naive assumption that theorists and researchers agreed on what sexual desire was and that there was a universally accepted definition of this phenomenon—a definition consistent with that provided by our research participant. However, our assumption proved incorrect. Not only do a variety of definitions of sexual desire pervade the theoretical and empirical literatures, but in addition, sexual desire often is confused with or considered equivalent to other aspects of human sexuality. We begin this chapter with an overview of the general phenomenon of desire, drawn primarily from Heider's (1958) classic treatise. We then apply this analysis to sexual desire, in the process distinguishing sexual desire from sexual arousal and sexual activity. Next, we consider the possibility that the experience of sexual desire can vary along a quantitative as well as a qualitative dimension. We end by reviewing the major theoretical conceptualizations and common operationalizations of sexual desire.

‍ Characteristics of a State of Desire

Psychologists have not neglected the general concept of desire. For example, the social psychologist Fritz Heider (1958) presented a classic discussion of the topic in *The Psychology of Interpersonal Relations*. According to Heider, desire is a motivational state that arises from within the person and that represents the person's own "wish" or "want." Desire is therefore a subjective, psychological condition that is not necessarily reflected by an individual's actual or potential actions:

> A wish may exist long before a specific action is taken to satisfy it, or without its ever being actualized in action. . . . a wish may exist even though no action on the part of the person is evident, either because no action is necessary, or because the person withholds action for certain reasons. (p. 128)

In addition, desire may have consequences other than overt, observable behaviors, such as the emotional reactions often associated with attaining or failing to attain the desired goal. Thus, although we often infer the existence of certain desires or motives from an individual's behavior, desire is not always directly manifested in behavior, and it cannot be directly linked with specific action patterns.

In a global sense, desire is directed toward a goal that the individual finds attractive or pleasurable. Indeed, although desire is not always linked to behavior, Heider argues that the fulfillment of desire is *always* linked to pleasure. That is, the desire for an event or object plus the attainment of said event or object leads to pleasure. This desire-pleasure connection is viewed as inviolable,

> meaning that wish-fulfillment *always* leads to pleasure, or, in the language of logic, that desire and obtaining *x* are sufficient conditions of pleasure. But, you may argue, what if the anticipated pleasure is not forthcoming? Is not this a common experience? Our reply is that even under these circumstances we never doubt for a moment that there is an a priori connection between desire and pleasure. Yet, if this connection is to be preserved, something must be doubted. As a matter of course, therefore, we either analyze the situation in an attempt to determine which of the underlying conditions is lacking, or we reappraise our reaction and conclude that our disappointment was unjustified. (pp. 130-131)

According to this perspective, an individual who desires X but is disappointed after obtaining X (a) did not actually desire X in the first place, (b) did desire X but the actual X obtained did not have the anticipated qualities, or (c) did desire X but was mistaken in his or her initial displeasure. Thus, if the desire for X really did exist and the individual really obtained what he or she desired, then pleasure will result. This desire-pleasure relation also can be understood within a cognitive framework. A person who desires X believes that the attainment of X will result in pleasure. Anticipated pleasure is therefore an important and essential component of desire.

Heider additionally notes that states of desire are characterized by a *separation* between the person and the valued object; that is, desire implies a certain distance between the individual and the desired object or objective. A similar notion can be found in an earlier work by American psychologist William James (1890/1950):

> Desire, wish, will, are states of mind which everyone knows, and which no definition can make plainer. We desire to feel, to have, to do, all sorts of things which at the moment are not felt, had, or done. (p. 486)

In sum, desire is conceptualized as a psychological state that reflects the awareness that one *wants* to be doing or feeling or having something that one is *not* now doing, feeling, or having and whose fulfillment is associated with pleasure.

❧ Characteristics of a State of Sexual Desire

Drawing on this earlier work, we might conceive of *sexual* desire as a psychological state subjectively experienced by the individual as an awareness that he or she wants or wishes to attain a (presumably pleasurable) sexual goal that is currently unattainable. Sexual desire, like other states of desire, is different from, although undoubtedly associated with, actual bodily responses. Interestingly, many researchers pay little attention to the distinction between the psychological state of sexual desire and other elements of human sexual response. → touch, visuals, etc.

Sexual Desire Distinguished From Sexual Arousal

Some researchers use the terms *sexual desire* and *sexual arousal* interchangeably (e.g., Abel, 1985; Dekker & Everaerd, 1989; Evans, 1989). However, sexual desire and sexual arousal are distinct experiences. Human sexual arousal contains both a physiological component and a psychological, or subjective, component. The former, *physiological-genital sexual arousal,* is usually conceptualized as a state of activation of a complex system of reflexes that involve the sex organs and the nervous system (e.g., Masters, Johnson, & Kolodny, 1982, 1994). Masters and Johnson (1966) were among the first to observe that during the arousal or "excitement" phase, both men and women undergo increased voluntary-muscle tension, increased heart rate, and elevated blood pressure. Additionally, women experience a vasocongestive increase in the diameter of the clitoral shaft, the appearance of vaginal lubrication, partial elevation of the uterus, and a minor thickening of the labia minora, and men experience the rapid occurrence of an erection, partial elevation of the testes, and flattening and elevation of the scrotal sac.

Physiological-genital sexual arousal may occur without conscious awareness. For example, not all women are able to subjectively report their current level of physiological-genital sexual arousal (e.g., Heiman, 1975). As a result, measures of physiological-genital sexual arousal do not rely on self-report but rather on direct assessment of physiological and genital events. In men, for example, physiological-genital sexual arousal frequently is assessed by monitoring penile circumference or tumescence with a mercury strain gauge placed along the penile shaft (e.g., Julien & Over, 1988; Rowland et al., 1987). Penile buckling force may also be measured for each episode of tumescence with a device consisting of a large rubber-capped syringe that has a sphygmomanometer at the other end—the buckling force represents the pressure being applied to the tip of the penis via the capped syringe when the erection first buckles or bends (e.g., Thase et al., 1988). Vaginal blood volume or blood volume pulse are the usual indicants of physiological-genital arousal in women (e.g., Adams, Haynes, & Brayer, 1985; Bohlen, Held, & Sanderson, 1983; Myers & Morokoff, 1986). These typically are measured by a photoplethysmograph, a tampon-shaped device that contains a small lamp, photocell, and connecting wires. After insertion into the vagina, the indirect light reflected back to the photocell from the vaginal wall responds to changes in vasocongestion, thereby enabling the researcher to assess blood flow responses to various (usually erotic) stimuli. Vaginal lubrication and labial or vaginal temperature also may be used as indicants of physiological-genital sexual arousal in women.

The second component of sexual arousal has been called *subjective sexual arousal* and is defined as the subjective awareness that one is genitally and physiologically aroused (e.g., Green & Mosher, 1985). In contrast to physiological-genital arousal, subjective sexual arousal can be assessed only via self-report. That is, subjective sexual arousal requires the individual's conscious awareness of sexual arousal:

> Subjective sexual arousal is conceived to be an affect-cognition blend, consisting of awareness of physiological sexual arousal, sexual affects, and affect-cognition blends, which is transmuted into consciousness and deepens involvement by amplifying the perception of sexual stimulation, sexual cognitions, sexual behavior, physi-

ological sexual response, and itself. (Mosher, Barton-Henry, & Green, 1988, p. 412)

Subjective sexual arousal typically is assessed via perceptions of genital or physiological changes that occur during exposure to sexual stimuli (e.g., conscious awareness of genital sensations, increased heart rate, perspiration) as well as through emotional or psychological responses to such changes. Specific operationalizations of subjective sexual arousal found in the literature include (a) subjective awareness of various genital sensations or reactions (e.g., breast sensations, vaginal lubrication, penile erection), (b) global self-report ratings of sexual arousal or sexual excitement, and (c) affect adjective checklists or rating scales that include terms ostensibly related to sexual arousal such as *passionate, lustful, horny, turned-on, sensual,* or *sexy* (e.g., Adams et al., 1985; Dekker, Everaerd, & Verhelst, 1985; Garcia, Brennan, DeCarlo, McGlennon, & Tait, 1984; Julien & Over, 1988; Mosher & Abramson, 1977; Mosher et al., 1988; Mosher & White, 1980; Przybyla & Byrne, 1984).

Sexual desire, as a psychological state, is clearly different from physiological-genital arousal, which is defined in terms of specific physiological and genital events that may occur without conscious awareness. However, it is easy to see why sexual desire might be confused with *subjective* sexual arousal. Both are subjective experiences and therefore both are assessed via self-report. Nonetheless, the subjective awareness that one is interested in sexual activities or stimuli, wishes to engage in sexual behavior, or craves sexual contact with another is arguably different from the subjective awareness that one is currently experiencing the physiological-genital indicants of sexual arousal, such as an erection, vaginal lubrication, or an elevated heart rate. Sexual desire implies the wish to obtain a sexual object that one does not now have or to engage in a sexual activity in which one is not now engaging. Subjective sexual arousal, on the other hand, is the awareness that one *is now* experiencing certain physiological and/or genital reactions. Both phenomena (i.e., sexual desire and subjective sexual arousal) can occur concurrently and also in the presence of physiological-genital arousal; however, sexual desire does not *depend* on physiological or genital reactions for its occurrence in the way that subjective sexual arousal does.

Sexual Desire Distinguished From Sexual Activity

Most researchers appear to agree that the occurrence of sexual activity does not necessarily imply the *desire* for sexual activity (e.g., Bancroft, Tennent, Loucas, & Cass, 1974; Brown, Monti, & Corriveau, 1978; Falicov, 1973; Schover, 1986; Wallen, 1990). However, some still assume that sexual behaviors such as intercourse serve as accurate indicants or measures of sexual desire. For example, during the process of validating the Sociosexual Orientation Inventory (SOI), Simpson and Gangestad (1991, Study 5) operationalized "general interest in sex" or "sex drive" (p. 876) as frequency of sexual activity in the past month (specifically, by asking couples to respond to the question, "How many times have you had sex (intercourse) in the past month?" p. 878). Frequency of intercourse, masturbatory activity, or other sexual behavior, however, does not constitute an adequate measure of sexual desire for several reasons.

First, of course, the occurrence of sexual activity does not necessarily imply a *desire* for such activity. Beck, Bozman, and Qualtrough (1991) asked college students whether they had ever been involved in sexual activity without sexual desire, and reported that the majority of both the men (60%) and women (82%) in their sample responded affirmatively. More recently, Regan (1997) asked a sample of undergraduates a similar question and reported that over half of the women and almost a fourth of the men stated that they had engaged in noncoercive but undesired sexual activities. Individuals may engage in sexual activity for a number of reasons other than for the satiation of their own sexual desire: They may do so to avoid rejecting their partner's advances and hurting their partner's feelings, to prove that they care for their partner and desire their partner sexually, to assure themselves of their own virility or sexual attractiveness, or to express feelings of closeness, warmth, commitment, and intimacy. Consider, for example, the following reasons given by a sample of men and women for engaging in casual sexual encounters (from Regan & Dreyer, in press):

> One night we had both been drinking and we got carried away and had sex. I didn't enjoy the actual act very much, but it did make me feel free and liberated from the long-term relationship I was previously in. I just needed to feel like I could explore sexually, without any ties or obligations, and I wanted to see what sex was like with another person. [female, age 22]

> Being drunk isn't really a cool reason, but we both were so I'm sure it had something to do with it. My partner was very willing—we share the same feelings about having sex for fun only with no strings attached. Her boyfriend was gone and I wasn't sure if another opportunity like this would come along. As long as proper precautions are taken, why not? Sex feels good. [male, age 20]

> I was going through a very insecure period where I wanted to have a relationship. At the time I thought that a one-night stand would be the right way to at least start developing one. I felt that sleeping with this particular person and sharing an intimate moment with him would be a good way to make him attracted to me and to want to go out with me. I wanted to feel loved. [female, age 20]

> Having sex is enjoyable and I was attracted to this person. Though on some social level, my friends expect and encourage this kind of behavior. Having sex with someone, especially if she's cute, gives you something to brag about and makes you more popular. It increases your self-confidence. So, the social conventions of my "sub-society" also add to my reasoning. [male, age 21]

Clearly, people have sex for motives sometimes only tangentially related to their own personal feelings of sexual desire.

Conversely, a lack of sexual activity does not necessarily reflect a lack of interest in such activity. For example, cultural proscriptions against intercourse and other forms of sexual activity during menstruation and pregnancy may result in a self- or partner-imposed abstinence that speaks more to social influence than to private inclination. Indeed, new mothers in an early 1973 study conducted by Kenny reported that they felt it was "safe" to resume sexual relations after childbirth only after their vaginal discharge ceased, even though they had experienced sexual desire prior to that time.

In addition, many sexual behaviors depend heavily on partner availability and willingness. Some researchers have attempted to circumvent this problem by expanding the list of sexual behaviors indicative of sexual interest to include autosexual activities such as masturbation (although this remains problematic insofar as some individuals are more comfortable or willing than others to engage in this form of sexual expression). Other researchers cleverly compose their samples of sexually active individuals who ostensibly have ready access to a sexual partner (e.g., married, engaged, or dating couples). However, an available partner does not necessarily imply a willing partner. That is, Joyce may experience sexual desire and attempt to initiate sexual intercourse with John but be rejected by him on the grounds that he is suffering from a headache. Alternately, Joyce may not experience sexual desire and therefore neither initiate nor engage in sexual intercourse with John. In both cases, sexual inter-course does not occur, and a researcher using this behavioral indicant would conclude that Joyce had not experienced sexual desire, was not interested in sex, or had a low sex drive—although in the first scenario, she did in fact experience sexual desire. In sum, sexual desire does not necessarily result in sexual activity; conversely, sexual activity does not necessarily imply the presence of sexual desire.

Dimensions of Sexual Desire

Although sexual desire is presumed to be distinct from physiologi-cal-genital sexual arousal, subjective sexual arousal, and sexual activity, these three experiences can—and frequently do—co-occur. For example, the sight of an attractive person may cause an individual to feel an urge to engage in sexual activities with that person and to fantasize about what sex with that person might be like; these desires may produce physiological and genital arousal. The subjective awareness of arousal may, in turn, increase the desire to engage in sex and may result in actual sexual behavior. After orgasm or sexual satiation, the body will return to its prearoused state, and sexual desire also may decrease. A variety of models of the interrelationship between desire, arousal, and activity are possible (for two examples, see DeLamater, 1991; Kaplan, 1979).

In addition, we believe that sexual desire varies along at least two dimensions. The first dimension is quantitative in nature and concerns the intensity and frequency of the sexual desire that is experienced. Any one individual may experience desire in varying intensities and at different frequencies. Krafft-Ebing (1886/1945) notes that "the existence of the sexual instinct is continuous during the time of sexual life, but it varies in intensity" (p. 26); similarly, any one person may experience sexual desire on numerous occasions one week, only to feel no desire the next. Levine (1987) also views fluctuations in intensity and frequency as one of the essential characteristics of sexual desire, and in his 1984 paper, he argues that the level of sexual desire experienced by adults may fluctuate along a spectrum of values ranging from "driven" to "avoidant." In addition, people may differ in the chronic amount (i.e., intensity and frequency) of sexual desire experienced. Kaplan (1979) argues that the sexual appetite of some individuals falls on the lower end of the sexual desire distribution as the result of various constitutional determinants, and Levine (1984) similarly notes that some individuals habitually occupy one end of the sexual desire spectrum.

The second dimension along which sexual desire varies is qualitative rather than quantitative and concerns the specificity of the desired objective (e.g., sexual activity) and object (e.g., person, inanimate object). An individual may experience a desire to engage in a specific or diffuse sexual activity with a specific or diffuse sexual object. For example, a bored, restless young man lying awake at night may experience a diffuse desire for sexual activity of some sort with a correspondingly diffuse object. That is, he wishes to engage in sexual activity, but his general state of interest has not crystallized into the shape of a particular interest in intercourse, masturbation, or other specific activity. The object of his desire is similarly diffuse; he wishes to engage in sexual activity but not necessarily with a specific person. However, if the young man desires to engage in sexual activity of some nature with his partner, he is experiencing desire for a diffuse objective with a specific object. Alternately, a woman watching a seduction scene from a late-night television show featuring her favorite actor may experience the desire to engage in intercourse with that particular individual (a specific objective with a specific object); alternately, she may simply experience the desire to engage in intercourse with an unspecified object (a specific objective with a diffuse object).

❧ Theoretical Approaches to Sexual Desire

There are two general frameworks to understanding sexual desire. The first, and most common view, contends that sexual desire is an innate motivational force (e.g., an instinct, drive, need, urge, appetite, wish, or want) that impels the individual to seek out sexual objects or to engage in sexual activities. This perspective emphasizes the appetitive, drivelike aspects and focuses on the intraindividual nature of sexual desire. The second view of sexual desire emphasizes the relational or interpersonal aspects of the phenomenon, conceptualizing desire as one factor in a larger relational context.

Motivational Views of Sexual Desire

As early as 1886, the German physician and founder of sexual pathology Richard von Krafft-Ebing (1886/1945) discussed sexual desire (also described as *libido sexualis*, "lust," and "longing for sexual satisfaction") as a potent "physiological law" (p. 25) that existed in humans as well as animals and that arose jointly from cerebral activity (e.g., use of the imagination) and the pleasurable physical sensations associated with this cerebral excitation:

> Sexual instinct—as emotion, idea and impulse—is a function of the cerebral *cortex*. Thus far no definite region of the cortex has been proved to be exclusively the seat of sexual sensations and impulses. This psychosexual centre is nothing more than a junction and crossing of principal paths which lead on the one hand to the sensitive motor apparatus of the sexual organs, and on the other hand to those nerve centres of the visual and olfactory organs which are the carriers of that consciousness which distinguishes between the "male" and the "female."

> Owing to the close relations which exist between the sexual instinct and the olfactory sense, it is to be presumed that the sexual and olfactory centres lie close together in the cerebral *cortex*. The development of sexual life has its beginning in the organic sensations which arise from the maturing reproductive glands. These excite the attention of the individual. Reading and the experiences of everyday life (which, unfortunately, are now-a-days too early and too frequently suggestive), convert these notions into clear ideas, which are accentuated by organic sensations of a pleasurable character.

> With this accentuation of erotic ideas through lustful feelings, an
> impulse to induce them is developed (sexual desire). (pp. 26-27)

The fact that Krafft-Ebing's work brought him into frequent contact
with sexual psychopaths, rapists, child molesters, and exhibitionists
increased his awareness of the power of the sexual forces that operated
within people and drove them to perform certain sexual acts, even in
the face of strong inhibitory social forces, and may have contributed
to his belief that "the gratification of the sexual instinct seems to be
the primary motive in man as well as in beast" (p. 2).

Freud, too, although operating from within a psychoanalytic framework, conceived of sexual desire—which is also called *libido*, or sexual
instinct—as a biological fact, an innate, motivational force analogous
to "the instinct of taking nourishment, and to hunger" (1905/1938,
p. 553):

> It is certainly not the case that the sexual instinct enters into children
> at the age of puberty in the way in which, in the Gospel, the devil
> entered into the swine. A child has its sexual instincts and activities
> from the first; it comes into the world with them; and, after an
> important course of development passing through many stages,
> they lead to what is known as the normal sexuality of the adult.
> (1910/1977, p. 42)

Arising from within the individual, sexual desire is conceptualized
as the psychic representation of a continually flowing inner somatic
source of stimulation that provides the impetus for sexual as well as
nonsexual actions.

Following in the footsteps of Krafft-Ebing and Freud, Helen Singer
Kaplan (e.g., 1977, 1979) states that sexual desire is an "appetite" or
"drive" that motivates us to engage in sexual behavior:

> Sexual desire is a drive that serves the biologic function of species
> survival. It instills a strong erotic hunger that prods us to engage in
> species specific behavior that leads to reproduction. It moves us to
> find a mate, to court, to seduce, to excite, to impregnate, to be
> impregnated. (1979, p. 78)

Like other drives, such as hunger, sexual desire is regulated by the
avoidance of pain and the seeking of pleasure, and it is produced by

the activation of a specific neural system in the brain. This neural system is presumed to contain centers that enhance the sexual drive in balance with centers that inhibit it and to have extensive connections with other parts of the brain, which allows the sexual drive to be influenced by and integrated into the individual's other life experiences. According to Kaplan (1979), sexual desire is primarily a *subjective* experience. Specifically:

> Sexual desire or libido is experienced as specific sensations which move the individual to seek out, or become receptive to, sexual experiences. These sensations are produced by the physical activation of a specific neural system in the brain. When this system is active, a person is "horny," he may feel genital sensations, or he may feel vaguely sexy, interested in sex, open to sex, or just even restless. These sensations cease after sexual gratification, i.e., orgasm. When this system is inactive or under the influence of inhibitory forces, a person has no interest in erotic matters; he "loses his appetite" for sex and becomes "asexual." (p. 10)

A similar view can be found in psychoanalyst Therese Benedek's (1977) earlier assertion that sexual desire or "the sexual instinct" (p. 53), is a subjective sexual experience that can be intensified into a driving need. Sex researchers Stuart, Hammond, and Pett (1987) conceptualize sexual desire as a biological drive subject to both endocrine fluctuations and the complex neural activity of the brain. They argue that these neurological and biochemical mechanisms may be influenced by psychological factors in the process of becoming translated into the subjective experience of desire. Similarly, Bancroft (1988) proposes that the heretofore elusive concept of sexual desire can be viewed as a subjective state similar to hunger. That is, a sexually "hungry" person experiences a subjective state that is labeled desire and he or she therefore is motivated to seek out and obtain sexual gratification in much the same way as a nutritionally deprived person experiences a subjective state that is labeled hunger and is motivated to obtain food. This "appetite for sex" (p. 11) is viewed as a complex interaction between cognitive processes, neurophysiological and biochemical mechanisms, and mood.

Other researchers, although not specifically defining sexual desire as a drive or appetite, also maintain that it has strong, drivelike properties. For example, Sherwin and Gelfand (1987) refer to sexual desire as one of "the motivational aspects of sexual behavior" (p. 398), and Schover (1986), although preferring to view desire as more akin to an interest in or anticipation of sexual activity rather than a drive such as hunger or thirst, agrees that the phenomenon contains motivational components. Still other researchers choose to define sexual desire not as a biological, innate motivational force per se but rather as a cognitive or emotional experience, such as wishing or longing, that reflects or is associated with the psychological experience of motivation. According to Schreiner-Engel, Schiavi, White, and Ghizzani (1989), sexual desire is best understood as a cognitive phenomenon that arises either spontaneously from within the individual or is externally stimulated by sensory (e.g., visual) erotic cues. Specifically, these researchers argue that sexual desire is the *wish* to engage in a sexual experience (p. 222). Everaerd (1988), on the other hand, defines sexual desire as an emotional experience that often is associated with action tendencies and that may blend with other emotional experiences.

An echo of these notions can be seen in the work of early motivation theorists who, although not interested in human sexuality per se, nevertheless sought to understand and specify the forces that governed human sexual and reproductive behavior. According to the majority of these theorists, sexual desire (i.e., sexual motivation, instinct, or appetite), can be understood as a psychological force that arises from biological needs and that impels or activates the organism to behave in a sexual manner. For example, Troland (1928) includes "lust" (also termed "erotic desire," "sexual impulse," and "sexual instinct") in his list of "fundamental instincts," and Holt (1931) speaks of a "sexual appetite" that, like other appetites, consists of "persistent afferent impulses coming from organs situated within the body" (p. 133) that increase in strength until the appetite is appeased. Moll (1933) argues that the "sex instinct" or "the instinct of reproduction" (p. 278) is the force that motivates the individual to engage in sexual activity and to reproduce: "The sex instinct of man and woman as well as that of higher animals is . . . a means of bringing together two cells, the sperm cell and the egg cell" (p. 278).

Similarly, although apologizing that "these details are a little unpleasant to discuss" (1890/1950, p. 439), William James states:

> Of all propensities, the sexual impulses bear on their face the most obvious signs of being instinctive, in the sense of blind, automatic, and untaught. The teleology they contain is often at variance with the wishes of the individuals concerned; and the actions are performed for no assignable reason but because Nature urges just that way. (p. 437)

According to James, sexual desire is a mental state that springs from the innate need to reproduce.

Like James, Dashiell (1928) seemed very aware of the impelling nature of the sexual urge:

> Food and sex are the great interests of the individual and of society. These may work out in various secondary forms, but the ground patterns of man's life are determined by these two elemental forces. This is, of course, an over-simplification of the story of the motivating of man's behavior; but it may be said that whereas the need of food, when extreme, may become most imperious, the urge to mating has played the most dramatic part in human history and is notorious for its power often to drive men through all barriers of individual inhibitions and of social taboos. (p. 236)

Tolman (1932) argued that various innate, fundamental, first-order drives or appetites provide the basis for all human behavior. Of the sexual appetite, he writes this:

> *Sex-hunger.* The initiating physiological state for this is an internal disequilibrium of glands and sex organs, and it provides a demand for the getting to a complementary physiological state of sexual quiescence—plus some very vague sign-gestalt-readiness, prior to tuition, as to how to achieve the latter, viz., intercourse with a sex-object, normal or perverted. The sexually excited individual demands sexual quiescence, and he releases a sign-gestalt-readiness to the effect that this demanded quiescence lies in the means-end-relation of intercourse with such and such types of sex object. He also releases a subordinate sign-gestalt-readiness that such a sex-object, if absent, is to be reached by exploring. (p. 277)

The personality psychologist Henry Murray and his colleagues (Murray et al., 1938) conceptualized the need for sex (*n* Sex) as a primary or viscerogenic need that seeks physical satisfaction (as opposed to mental or emotional satisfaction), is directed toward the enjoyment of sensations such as "erotic excitement" (p. 167), and forces the organism toward other objects. Specifically, *n* Sex motivates the individual "to form and further an erotic relationship. To have sexual intercourse" (p. 167). Feelings associated with this need were said to include erotic excitement, lust, and love, and persons with a high need for sex were described as frequently thinking about sexual matters, losing themselves in sexual fantasies, and believing themselves to have a strong sexual instinct.

According to Bertocci's (1988) theory of motivation, "lust-sex" is a primary emotion (i.e., appetitive tendency, instinct, or unlearned, constitutive human motive) that involves both organic, physiological processes and psychosocial learning processes. Bertocci argues that human sexual motivation is a subjective experience that directs the person toward various sexual objects, including same- or opposite-sex individuals, animals, or inanimate objects, and that can be initiated, sustained, and gratified by various behavioral, imaginary, and symbolic sexual actions:

> Lust-sex is the emotion experienced by a person as a qualitative impetus whose meaning-objective is usually a member of the opposite sex deemed attractive in ways that facilitate sexual advances and intercourse. (p. 222)

Similarly, Evans (1989) defines sexual desire or sexual motivation as a psychological concept that reflects "the extent to which [humans] pursue sexual goals" (p. 28) and that results from both biologically based, hormonal mechanisms and higher cortical activity, and Lichtenberg (1989) discusses a universal, psychological entity he labels the "sensual-sexual motivational system" that is present at birth and that is built around the separate but related needs for sensual enjoyment and sexual excitement.

All of the aforementioned theorists and researchers emphasize the intraindividual nature of sexual desire. That is, some innate biological need arising from within the body (and considered by some to be subject to learning and socialization processes) produces a subjective state of "sexual desire" that impels the individual to seek out or become receptive to sexual objects and/or experiences.

Relational Views of Sexual Desire.

Other investigators, however, have suggested that desire is best viewed as an entirely *externally* generated phenomenon. For example, Verhulst and Heiman (1979) conclude that "desire is the experience of, interest in, and attraction to, the partner as a sexual being. One could say desire is located in the partner rather than in oneself, since it is a feeling of being drawn to the other" (p. 21). Here, sexual desire originates from an external source of stimulation located within the desired object rather than from some need arising within the desiring individual. Interestingly, current approaches to the treatment of sexual desire disorders are beginning to recognize the potent influence of the external environment—for example, the relationship between a person and his or her sexual partner—on the individual's experience of sexual desire. Many clinicians, therefore, have begun to conceptualize and evaluate sexual desire from a more situationally based perspective (e.g., Arnett, Prosen, & Toews, 1986; Fish, Fish, & Sprenkle, 1984; Pietropinto, 1986; Regas & Sprenkle, 1984; Schover, 1986; Talmadge & Talmadge, 1986). Regas and Sprenkle (1984) even propose a systems-behavioral model of therapeutic intervention that focuses on the afflicted individual's interactions with the sexual partner in defining and determining sexual desire. Sexual desire thus is viewed as part of a larger relational system rather than merely one aspect of individual sexual response.

Levine's Integrative Model of Sexual Desire

As can be seen from the preceding review, comprehensive, explanatory theories that specify the causal antecedents and consequences of sexual desire are almost nonexistent; rather, the majority of researchers have focused on defining sexual desire. Levine (e.g., 1984, 1987), however, has proposed one such integrative model. Levine argues that sexual desire is generated and influenced by both internal and external events. According to his model, sexual desire is an intensely personal subjective experience that can be defined as "the psychobiologic energy that precedes and accompanies arousal and tends to produce sexual behavior" (1987, p. 36). Although ideally experienced by the individual as a unitary phenomenon, Levine believes that desire is best viewed as the product of an interaction among (a) the neuroendocrine system, which yields a biologically based, sexual drive; (b) the cognitive processes that generate the wish to behave sexually; and (c) the psychologically based, motivational processes that result in the willingness to behave sexually. Changes in any of these three constituents influence the likelihood that an individual will feel sexual desire and also affect the intensity of his or her experience. Thus, the biologically based, sexual drive can be diminished by factors such as mental or physical illness, age, grief, and drugs. The cognitive wish to behave sexually may be stimulated by the desire to feel loved or valued, to feel masculine or feminine, or to please one's partner; conversely, the cognitive wish *not* to behave sexually may stem from a fear of disease or pregnancy or from the conviction that sex is morally wrong. Finally, the motivational willingness to behave sexually may be enhanced or diminished by the verbal or nonverbal behavior of the sexual partner, voyeuristic experiences, the quality of the nonsexual relationship with the partner, previous relationships and interpersonal attachments, and so forth. In other words, the presence or absence of these and other variables creates an environment that is—or is not—conducive to the experience of sexual desire. For example, a physically and mentally healthy person who experiences spontaneous manifestations of genital excitement (high biological drive), who believes that these feelings are appropriate in the context of the current relationship and who is motivated to share them with the partner (high cognitive wish), and who has a history of positive interpersonal sexual experiences (high motivation or willingness) is likely to experience sexual desire. That same individual is much less likely to feel desire if the partner verbally expresses a lack of sexual interest (which hinders motivation), even in the presence of drive and/or cognitive wish.

One of the major strengths of Levine's model is that it allows for the integration of both internal and external determinants of sexual desire. That is, although sexual desire is subjectively experienced by the individual alone, it represents the product of purely internal, intrapsychic components such as drive and the conscious intent to seek sexual stimulation with such externally derived components as interpersonal attraction and past relationship experiences. We will discuss research on several of these internal and external causes of sexual desire in subsequent chapters.

ᴥ The Measurement of Sexual Desire

How a researcher measures, or operationalizes, sexual desire naturally depends on how he or she defines it. Many researchers who wish to assess desire for sexual activity directly ask their participants about *sexual desire* or *sexual interest* (frequency, level, degree, or amount). Others employ such motivationally oriented euphemisms as *sexual motivation*, *sex drive*, *sexual urge*, *sexual craving*, and *sexual appetite*. Some researchers refer to the Freudian motivational concept of *libido*, a potentially problematic practice if participants do not interpret this term to mean sexual desire. Many researchers do, however, explicitly define libido as erotic or sexual desire or interest (e.g., Benedek & Rubenstein, 1939a, 1939b; Greenblatt, Mortara, & Torpin, 1942; Huffer, Levin, & Aronson, 1970; McCoy & Davidson, 1985). In other instances, libido is assumed to reflect the subjective experiential component of the human sexual response, insofar as it is distinguished from physiological sexual responses. For example, Burger et al. (1984) explicitly differentiate libido from sexual enjoyment and orgasm, and Appelt and Strauss (1986) make a similar distinction between libido, sexual arousal, and orgasm for their respondents.

Other researchers attempting to measure sexual desire have operationalized the concept in terms of cognitive events (e.g., *sexual wishes, sexual thoughts, sexual fantasies, sexual imagery*) not associated with any overt sexual activity under the assumption that these phenomena represent motivational aspects of sexual experience and therefore may serve as indirect measures of sexual desire (e.g., Sherwin, 1985; Wilson, 1988). The fact that both men and women who seek treatment for low sexual desire also fantasize less during sexual activity and general daydreaming than do individuals with normal desire levels lends support to this assumption (e.g., Nutter & Condron, 1983, 1985).

A final operational category includes psychological events such as *sexual feelings* not associated with any overt sexual activity and not meant to include genital sensations and *sexual attraction* or an attraction to another individual that is explicitly based on sexual feelings.

✿ Conclusions

The goal of this chapter was to consider the phenomenon of sexual desire—what it is, how it is different from other sexual experiences, along what dimensions it varies, and how it is measured. What can we conclude? First, sexual desire is presumed to be produced and influenced both by intraindividual (i.e., organic or biological) and by external (i.e., relational) factors. Second, sexual desire is a subjective, psychological experience or motivational state that can be understood broadly as an interest in sexual objects or activities, or as a wish, longing, or craving to seek out sexual objects or to engage in sexual activities. Third, this experience is distinct from physiological/genital sexual arousal (i.e., a state of reflex activation that involves the sex organs and nervous system), subjective sexual arousal (i.e., the subjective awareness of physiological/genital arousal), and sexual activity (e.g., masturbation, intercourse). Sexual desire, arousal, and activity may co-occur, but the latter do not themselves constitute adequate indicants of sexual desire. Fourth, sexual desire may vary both in terms of its intensity and frequency and commonly in terms of the specificity of the goal it seeks. Finally, sexual desire commonly is operationalized as a motivational (e.g., drive, instinct, urge, craving, want) or cognitive (e.g., wish, thought, fantasy) construct and typically is assessed via self-report.

In coming to these conclusions, we drew heavily on both general desire theory and specific theoretical approaches to sexual desire. However, most researchers interested in sexual desire have followed an atheoretical, empirical approach. Rather than concern themselves with defining what sexual desire is, they instead have focused on the various factors that seem to be associated with the presence or absence of sexual desire. Of these, intraindividual or personal characteristics have received the most attention. In the next several chapters, we turn to this literature.

3

Sexual Desire
The Body (Part I)

A number of empirical attempts have been made to delineate and explore the correlates and presumed causal antecedents of sexual desire. The majority of researchers have focused on causes located within or under the control of the individual. In the next two chapters, we review the physical causes and correlates of sexual desire—the "body" of sexual desire. Of these presumed intraindividual, physical causes of sexual desire, hormones and hormonal processes have received the lion's share of empirical attention. Certainly, human sexuality is less biologically determined and more volitional than any reference to "raging hormones" or "puberty-stricken, sex-starved teenagers" would have us believe. Nonetheless, many young adults believe that biological and hormonal processes cause sexual desire in men and women (Regan & Berscheid, 1995), and research strongly indicates that both endogenous and exogenous hormones contribute at least partially to the timing and magnitude of this particular aspect of sexuality. It is therefore to these factors that we turn in the present chapter.

In the first half of the chapter, we examine what has been empirically established about the relationship between the sex hormones and sexual desire as experienced by men and women. The discussion of each sex hormone includes an overview of the endocrine glands associated with the production of that hormone, the major naturally occurring forms of the hormone, the amounts typically present in the blood plasma of adult men and women, and the relation between the hormone and sexual desire. We wish to note that, because androgens and prolactin appear to have a similar relationship to desire in both men and women, the sections on those hormones have been organized according to effect on sexual desire (i.e., increase, decrease, none) rather than by sex or gender (i.e., effect on men, effect on women), to avoid unnecessary redundancy. However, the discussions of sexual desire and estrogens and progesterone are organized according to sex or gender, primarily because the research in both these areas involving the impact of these sex hormones on male sexuality is relatively sparse. The second half of the chapter explores the association between feelings of sexual desire and female life events that are hormonally mediated (i.e., the menstrual cycle, pregnancy, menopause).

We adhered to the following guidelines when selecting articles for inclusion in this and subsequent review chapters. We included articles whose authors (a) specifically mentioned *sexual desire* or *sexual interest* in the body of their article and/or included these terms in the measures administered to their participants, (b) invoked terms such as *sexual motivation, sex or sexual drive, sexual appetite,* and *libido* but were clearly referring to sexual desire, or (c) indirectly assessed sexual desire by using an operationalization that adequately reflects the construct of sexual desire (e.g., subjective, psychological sexual experiences such as sexual thoughts, sexual wishes, sexual feelings, sexual cravings, sexual attraction). At all times, we have attempted to clearly state the specific operationalizations of desire employed by each researcher.

❧ Hormones

Androgens

Androgens, or masculinizing hormones, are primarily synthesized in the testes and the adrenal cortex (the outer section of the adrenal glands) and to a lesser extent in the ovaries. The primary naturally occurring androgens are testosterone, androstenedione, and dehydroepiandrosterone, and under normal circumstances, a man's bloodstream contains a much greater overall quantity of these hormones than does a woman's bloodstream (Brooks, 1984; Naik & Pennington, 1981). For example, average values for plasma testosterone concentrations in healthy adult men fall within the range of 300 to 1500 nanograms per 100 milliliters of plasma (ng/100 ml), whereas in premenopausal women the levels range from 14 to 176 ng/100 ml throughout the menstrual cycle. Mean plasma levels for androstenedione, however, are higher in women than in men, ranging between 112 to 200 ng/100 ml during the menstrual cycle compared with the lower 60 ng/100 ml typically present in male plasma.

A growing body of evidence indicates that sexual desire is to some extent androgen dependent in both men and women (e.g., Davidson, Camargo, & Smith, 1979; O'Carroll & Bancroft, 1984; Sherwin, 1988; Skakkebaek, Bancroft, Davidson, & Warner, 1981; Waxenberg, Finkbeiner, Drellich, & Sutherland, 1960). For example, Persky and colleagues (1982) demonstrated that both testosterone and androstenedione were significantly and negatively correlated with their female participants' "sexual avoidance" scores, defined by the researchers as the null of sexual desire. Udry, Billy, Morris, Groff, and Raj (1985) determined that free testosterone levels predicted the frequency of sexual thoughts experienced by adolescent boys better than six other hormones, pubertal development, and age. A more recent study conducted by Halpern, Udry, Campbell, Suchindran, and Mason (1994) similarly found a positive correlation between free testosterone levels and frequency of sexual thoughts in adolescent boys.

The proposed relationship between endogenous androgens and sexual functioning also has been examined via women who have undergone surgical procedures such as oophorectomy (removal of the ovaries) and adrenalectomy (removal of the adrenal glands) that result in a sudden and uniform decrease in circulating levels of plasma testosterone and estrogen. In one of the first attempts to examine this relationship, Waxenberg, Drellich, and Sutherland (1959) conducted a study in which they interviewed 29 women diagnosed with metastatic breast cancer who had undergone total bilateral oophorectomy and adrenalectomy. Of the 17 who reported some consciousness of sexual desire prior to adrenalectomy, 10 (58.8%) reported a total loss of desire and 4 (23.5%) reported a noticeable decrease in desire after the procedure. In addition, interviews with the 7 women who had undergone oophorectomy 16 to 60 months prior to adrenalectomy allowed the researchers to compare the effects of the loss of a major source of estrogens with the effects of the loss of a major source of androgens. Results indicated that removal of the ovaries in and of themselves decreased but did not critically alter the participants' experience of sexual desire; rather, sexual desire underwent a significant reduction only subsequent to removal of the adrenal glands. Although this pioneering study has been criticized for its lack of an experimental control group, its extremely limited sample size, and its use of a physically traumatized participant population, the results strongly suggest that adrenal androgens do influence what Waxenberg et al. (1959) term the "erotic component" of sexuality.

Indeed, treatment with synthetic steroids that suppress the synthesis of testosterone and interfere with the activity of the adrenal androgens has reliably been associated with diminished sexual interest and desire in at least three groups of individuals: Sex offenders, prostate cancer patients, and women suffering from various androgen-dependent hair and skin conditions. Antiandrogenic substances such as cyproterone (CPA) and medroxyprogesterone (MPA) acetate were originally developed for use as oral contraceptives and to treat various gynecologic disorders, but they have been most widely used and recognized as a treatment for sex offenders and other individuals unable to control socially or personally unacceptable sexual urges and dysfunctional sexual desires. Men treated with CPA or MPA have reported a reduction in their frequency of sexual thoughts, erotic fantasies, and sexual "urges" (e.g., Bancroft et al., 1974; Berlin & Meinecke, 1981; Cooper, Ismail, Phanjoo, & Love, 1972; Hucker, Langevin, & Bain, 1988; Kravitz et al., 1995; Young, 1987). Marked decreases in sexual desire also have been noted in prostate cancer patients who received antiandrogenic treatment in combination with medical or surgical castration as a means of completely depriving cancerous cells of the stimulation provided by the adrenal sex steroids (e.g., Labrie et al., 1986; Rousseau, DuPont, Labrie, & Couture, 1988). Similarly, although the use of androgen antagonists generally is viewed as a viable and reasonably successful form of treatment for androgen-dependent hair and skin problems (e.g., acne, alopecia, hirsutism, seborrhea), some researchers have noted a loss of "libido" as one of the substances' various sexual side effects (e.g., Appelt & Strauss, 1986; Cittadini & Barreca, 1977; Cremoncini, Vignati, & Libroia, 1977; Hammerstein, Meckies, Leo-Rosberg, Moltz, & Zielske, 1975). Unfortunately, the majority of these researchers do not provide a more specific definition of *libido*, and therefore we cannot know for certain whether the results point to an effect of decreased androgen production on sexual desire per se.

Not only does a decrease in the level of circulating androgens (whether brought about by surgical procedures such as oophorectomy and adrenalectomy or by the administration of antiandrogenic steroids such as CPA and MPA) reliably result in a diminution of sexual desire in both men and women, but an *increase* in androgen level yields an associated increase in sexual interest or desire. The administration of exogenous androgens (usually testosterone) to men and women complaining of low sexual interest has been noted to result in an increase in the self-reported strength of sexual desire (Rabkin, Rabkin, & Wagner, 1995) and in the frequency of sexual thoughts (O'Carroll & Bancroft, 1984) and desire for intercourse (Greenblatt et al., 1942; Kennedy, 1973; Salmon & Geist, 1943). Androgen replacement therapy also has been successfully used to increase the self-reported frequency of sexual thoughts and feelings (Kwan, Greenleaf, Mann, Crapo, & Davidson, 1983; O'Carroll, Shapiro, & Bancroft, 1985; Skakkebaek et al., 1981) and the sexual desire (Kennedy, 1973; Kwan et al., 1983; Salmimies, Kockott, Pirke, Vogt, & Schill, 1982) of men with hypogonadism or eugonadism (conditions caused by various disorders of the endocrine system that result in abnormally low levels of testosterone and, if occurring before puberty, the failure to develop normal adult secondary sex characteristics).

Similar results have been obtained in women. Kaplan and Owett (1993) describe the spontaneous return of "libido" and "sexual feelings" in a sample of 7 women with androgen deficiency syndrome (i.e., a demonstrable androgen deficiency caused by chemotherapy with cytotoxic agents and/or bilateral salpingo-oophorectomies) after testosterone replacement therapy. Combined subcutaneous implants of testosterone and the estrogenic hormone estradiol also have been associated with significant increases in women's sexual interest, sexual desire, and libido, as well as in the number of sexual thoughts and fantasies (e.g., Brincat et al., 1984; Burger et al., 1984; Cardozo et al., 1984; Sherwin, 1985; but see Dow & Gallagher, 1989; Slob et al., 1993). Although the design of the latter studies does not permit discrimination between the effects of testosterone and estradiol, it is interesting to note that the libido of Burger et al.'s (1984) participants was neither noticeably affected nor improved by an earlier treatment with oral estrogens. In addition, an appropriately controlled investigation conducted by Sherwin, Gelfand, and Brender (1985) clearly suggests that it is the exogenous testosterone rather than the estradiol that contributes to enhanced sexual desire. These investigators gave injections of an androgenic, estrogenic, androgenic-estrogenic combined, or placebo preparation to premenopausal women who required a hysterectomy and oophorectomy for reasons other than malignant disease. The study began with an initial 3-month treatment phase in which each woman was randomly assigned to receive one of the four preparations, continued through a 1-month placebo phase, and concluded with a second treatment phase in which each woman received one of the treatments to which she had not previously been exposed. Hormonal assay and analysis of daily ratings made by the participants indicated that women who received either the androgenic or androgenic-estrogenic combined preparation not only developed significantly higher levels of plasma testosterone but experienced higher levels of sexual desire and reported a greater number of sexual fantasies during both of the treatment phases than did those women who received the estrogenic drug or the placebo. In addition, withdrawal of treatment during the intervening placebo month was associated with simultaneous decreases in plasma testosterone levels, sexual desire scores, and frequency of sexual fantasies in both androgen-treated groups. This well-controlled study, along with the other results reviewed above, certainly provides support for the hypothesis that sexual desire is to some extent androgen dependent.

Exactly how critical a role, however, do androgens play in the experience of sexual desire? Certainly testosterone and other androgens appear to influence desire, but are they necessary for desire to occur? Researchers are currently exploring the possibility that only a minimum amount of androgenic substance need be present in the hormonal environment for desire to be experienced. For example, Sherwin (1988; also see Bancroft, 1988) proposed that sexual desire will be noticeably affected only when the level of hormone has dropped below some unspecified critical threshold; at or above this threshold, increasing levels of hormone will have no further influence on desire. This notion would help explain why the serum testosterone levels of the physically healthy men in a study conducted by Brown and colleagues (1978) failed to correlate significantly with the daily frequency of sexual thoughts and sexual interest—the majority of healthy men have more testosterone than is required for the experience of sexual desire. The same may be true for women. Bancroft, Sanders, Davidson, and Warner (1983) discovered that the testosterone levels of the women in their study were highly correlated with sexual activities such as masturbation but were negatively or insignificantly correlated with subjective measures such as sexual feelings and pleasant sexual thoughts. Similarly, the mean adrenal levels of the older, post-menopausal women in the Persky et al. (1982) study were significantly lower than those of the premenopausal women, although both groups of women reported the same levels of sexual desire.

The above results suggest that the presence of some specified level of androgens may be *necessary* for the experience of sexual desire. However, at least two hormonal examinations of physically healthy women diagnosed with hypoactive sexual desire disorder (HSD) or inhibited sexual desire (ISD) suggest that androgens alone are not *sufficient* for sexual desire. A radioimmunoassay conducted by Stuart et al. (1987) of blood samples collected from ISD and non-ISD women revealed no significant differences with regard to mean testosterone levels, although members of the non-ISD group were more dissatisfied with their current mean monthly frequency of intercourse and desired a greater mean frequency than the ISD women. (We should point out, however, that these results are themselves somewhat ambiguous insofar as the desired frequency of intercourse may or may not reflect the frequency of sexual desire; that is, "I want to have sex

10 times a month" is not necessarily the same thing as "10 times a month I experience a desire to have sex").

Similarly, Schreiner-Engel and colleagues (1989) found no significant differences between 17 women who met DSM-III-R criteria for HSD and 13 healthy, sexually functional women in mean endocrine values sampled within each of three consecutive menstrual cycle phases; in the menstrual cycle variation of testosterone, estradiol, progesterone, and prolactin; and in the follicular or luteal values of bioavailable testosterone. Significant differences were obtained, however, in levels of subjectively experienced sexual desire; specifically, the non-HSD group expressed a greater frequency of interest in and desire for sex and experienced a greater number of sexual thoughts and fantasies. Apparently, more than circulating levels of testosterone influences whether an individual will experience sexual desire.

Indeed, Carney, Bancroft, and Mathews (1978) discovered that sexually dysfunctional women who received testosterone in conjunction with counseling reported a greater increase in the number of sexual thoughts experienced on a weekly basis than did women who completed a program consisting of counseling and an anxiety-reducing drug (diazepam). However, the failure of subsequent researchers to replicate these results (e.g., Mathews, Whitehead, & Kellet, 1983) suggests that testosterone (at least in the dosage used by Mathews et al., 1983) alone is insufficient to produce increases in sexual desire.

In sum, sexual desire appears to be somewhat androgen dependent. That is, a certain critical level of these hormones seems necessary, although not sufficient, for the experience of sexual desire in both men and women.

Estrogens

The feminizing hormones known as estrogens are largely secreted by the ovaries, with lesser amounts manufactured in the adrenal cortex, peripheral tissues (e.g., fat, muscle, kidney, liver, hypothalamus), and in men, the testes. The placenta is a major source of estrogens during pregnancy (Baird, 1976). The primary naturally occurring estrogenic hormone is estradiol, although its weaker and less active counterparts, estrone and estriol, also are considered to have important effects on human sexual function (Fotherby, 1984;

Mazenod, Pugeat, & Forest, 1988; Naik & Pennington, 1981). In pre-menopausal women, plasma levels of estradiol and estrone generally greatly exceed concentrations found in male plasma. Specifically, throughout the menstrual cycle, estradiol levels range from 30 to 570 picograms per milliliter of plasma (pg/ml); in men, plasma concentrations of estradiol range from 10 to 30 pg/ml. Estrone levels tend to range from 30 to 220 pg/ml in women and from 10 to 70 pg/ml in men.

The role of such estrogens as estradiol and estrone in male sexual interest and desire has yet to be clearly delineated, although there is some evidence that heightened total estrogen levels may result in decreased sexual desire. For example, the administration of exogenous estrogenic preparations appears to be somewhat effective in reducing the sexual interest and fantasies of sex offenders and men who engage in deviant sexual behavior or who suffer from uncontrollable sexual urges (e.g., Bancroft et al., 1974; Cooper, 1986; Field & Williams, 1970; Golla & Hodge, 1949; Whittaker, 1959). This treatment, however, has been associated with a potpourri of deleterious side effects, including nausea, vomiting, feminization, and even breast cancer (e.g., Cooper, 1986; Field & Williams, 1970; Golla & Hodge, 1949; Symmers, 1968; Tennent, Bancroft, & Cass, 1974), that in themselves may have a negative impact on the desire to seek out and engage in sexual activity.

Although male sexual desire is presumed to be adversely affected by higher levels of estrogens, some researchers argue that the presence of estrogens (particularly estradiol) is necessary for normal sexual desire in women (e.g., Benedek & Rubenstein, 1939a, 1939b). However, the majority of evidence suggests that these hormones have little direct influence on that aspect of female sexuality (e.g., Campbell, 1976; Campbell & Whitehead, 1977; Coope, 1976; Furuhjelm, Karlgren, & Carlstrom, 1984; Kane, Lipton, & Ewing, 1969; Leiblum, Bachmann, Kemmann, Colburn, & Schwartzman, 1983; Schreiner-Engel, Schiavi, Smith, & White, 1981; Sherwin, 1985; Studd et al., 1977; Waxenberg et al., 1960; also see Kaplan, 1992). Recall that Schreiner-Engel et al. (1989) found no significant differences in levels of estradiol between 17 women with hypoactive sexual desire disorder and 13 healthy, sexually functional women, even though the two groups differed significantly in terms of levels of subjectively experienced sexual desire. In addition, research on the sexual experience of women undergoing menopause indicates that although sexual desire may decrease after the ovaries cease to function, this decline is not necessarily estrogen dependent (e.g., Bancroft, 1988). Similarly, the sexual desire of premenopausal women who undergo oophorectomy does not appear to be critically altered by the loss of a major source of estrogens (e.g., Filler & Drezner, 1944; Waxenberg et al., 1959).

The administration of exogenous estrogenic compounds to women suffering from various gynecologic disorders or menopausal symptoms also does not usually affect sexual desire (e.g., Burger et al., 1984; Furuhjelm et al., 1984; Salmon & Geist, 1943; Sherwin et al., 1985; but see Dennerstein & Burrows, 1982; Dennerstein, Burrows, Wood, & Hyman, 1980). Salmon and Geist (1943) treated 30 women who experienced diminished desire associated with menopause, oophorectomy, or gynecological disturbances such as amenorrhea with either an estrogen, an androgen, or an estrogen and an androgen simultaneously. Not one of the 11 women who received the estrogen-alone treatment reported a resurgence of her desire for intercourse, although 8 who had previously noted painful intercourse caused by vaginitis and a subsequent disinterest in that activity did experience relief from both the vaginal symptom and coital discomfort. When an androgen was substituted for the estrogenic preparation, however, all but one of this subsample noticed an appreciable increase in sexual desire. Consistent with these results, the surgically menopausal women in Sherwin et al.'s (1985) study, discussed above, who received an estrogenic preparation (as opposed to an androgenic, androgenic-estrogenic combined, or placebo preparation) reported the lowest levels of sexual desire and the fewest sexual fantasies, even though their plasma estrogen levels during both treatment phases were as high as those of the androgen-estrogen combined group.

In sum, it remains possible that estrogenic hormones indirectly affect female sexual desire by preventing and relieving vaginal symptoms (e.g., dryness, lack of elasticity) that often result in painful intercourse and that may contribute to diminished interest in sexual activity. However, it seems more likely that these hormones are not causally related to sexual desire in men or women.

Progesterone

This sex hormone is primarily produced by the ovaries (and, during pregnancy, the placenta), with lesser amounts manufactured in the adrenal cortex and testes. In premenopausal, healthy women, progesterone concentrations range from mean levels of 31 to 1,550 ng/100 ml during the course of the menstrual cycle. These levels are higher than those seen in normal, healthy men, for whom plasma concentrations range from between 19 and 30 ng/100 ml.

Much of the research in this area has focused on the effect of progesterone on the sexual desire of women; as a result, very little is known about the influence of this hormone on male sexuality. However, some evidence indicates that progesterone may have a dampening effect on male sexual desire. For example, in an uncontrolled study, Heller, Laidlaw, Harvey, and Nelson (1958) noted decreased libido in 4 males receiving intramuscular progesterone, and progesterone has also been used to treat hypersexuality or reduce excessive sexual desire and urges in men (Money, 1970).

Some researchers speculate that exogenous progesterone may have a similar inhibitory impact on sexual interest in women (e.g., Bancroft, 1984, 1988; Benedek & Rubenstein, 1939a, 1939b; Greenblatt, McCall, & Torpin, 1941; McCauley & Ehrhardt, 1976). Indeed, the use of oral contraceptives that elevate progesterone throughout the cycle has been linked with decreased sexual interest and desire (e.g., Huffer et al., 1970; Kane et al., 1969; Warner & Bancroft, 1988; but see McCullough, 1974). In addition, subfacially implanted progesterone pellets used to treat a variety of gynecological disorders have been associated with a marked reduction in sexual desire (e.g., Greenblatt et al., 1942).

Still other research, however, suggests that progesterone has no demonstrable effect on female sexual interest (e.g., Abplanalp, Rose, Donnelly, & Livingstone-Vaughan, 1979; Schreiner-Engel et al., 1989). Schreiner-Engel et al. (1989) found no significant differences in the menstrual cycle variation of progesterone between groups of sexually dysfunctional and sexually functional women, although those in the functional group expressed a greater frequency of interest in and desire for sex and experienced a greater number of sexual thoughts and fantasies.

To further complicate matters, exogenously administered progesterone has been noted to *increase* desire in women under certain circumstances. Bakke (1965) reported that 11 of a sample of 27 hysterectomized, menopausal women who were administered an estrogenic preparation, a combined estrogen and progestin preparation, and a placebo in a random sequence noticed an increase in sexual interest while on the combined pill that was substantially greater than anything experienced while taking the estrogen-alone or placebo pills.

The effect of progesterone on human sexual desire, then, is not clear; it may adversely affect male sexual desire, and it may or may not increase or decrease female sexual desire.

Prolactin

Prolactin is produced by the pituitary gland. Mean levels of this hormone tend to range from approximately 9 to 18 ng/ml in women and 5 to 14 ng/ml in men, although normal serum levels for healthy adults of both sexes are generally defined as equal to or less than 30 ng/ml. In women, the lactational period following pregnancy and delivery is characterized by elevated levels of prolactin and often suppression of ovarian activity and resulting lowered levels of progesterone and estrogen. Prolactin levels also tend to increase slightly at ovulation, and prolactin levels in both men and women appear subject to a diurnal rhythm in which they rise after the onset of sleep and peak in the early morning (Pennington, Naik, & Bevan, 1981).

Most research involving prolactin has focused on behavioral or physiological aspects of sexual function (e.g., intercourse, erection, and ejaculation in men and intercourse and orgasm in women; for reviews see Drago, 1984; Muller, Musch, & Wolf, 1979). Some researchers, however, have reported an association between elevated prolactin levels and decreased sexual desire. For example, men and women with hyperprolactinemia, a condition characterized by prolactin levels greater than 30 to 35 ng/ml, frequently report a decrease in sexual interest that subsequently improves when their prolactin levels are reduced by treatment with, for example, bromocriptine (a dopamine agonist that lowers levels of plasma prolactin; e.g., Bancroft, 1984; Bancroft, O'Carroll, McNeilly, & Shaw, 1984; Buckman & Kellner, 1985;

Muller et al., 1979; Riley, 1984; Schwartz, Bauman, & Masters, 1982). Chronic renal failure is frequently associated with both hyperprolactinemia and decreased sexual desire, and men and women effectively treated for the hormonal abnormality tend to report a restoration of their lost interest (e.g., Weizman et al., 1983). Similarly, although many studies involving lactating women have focused on the relation between sexual interest and physiological changes such as altered breast sensitivity and size rather than on hormonal changes (e.g., Hames, 1980), some researchers report that lactating women, like many individuals with elevated prolactin levels, also experience less sexual desire than when not nursing. For example, Kayner and Zagar (1983) found that the majority (62.6%) of their sample of 121 presently or recently lactating women reported experiencing less or no sexual desire while nursing compared with prepregnancy levels.

This pattern, however, is far from universal. Some men and women with hyperprolactinemia do not experience a loss of sexual interest, and some of those who do fail to find their difficulties alleviated by a form of treatment that successfully reduces prolactin levels (see, for example, Franks, Jacobs, Martin, & Nabarro, 1978; Koppelman, Parry, Hamilton, Alagna, & Loriaux, 1987). For that matter, a normal prolactin level does not ensure the presence of sexual desire; hormonal assays have revealed normal prolactin levels in women who report low frequencies of interest in and desire for sex, experience a decreased number of sexual thoughts and fantasies, and express strong dissatisfaction with their perceived low monthly frequency of intercourse (e.g., Alder, Cook, Davidson, West, & Bancroft, 1986; Schreiner-Engel et al., 1989; Stuart et al., 1987). In addition, some data now suggest that the increased levels of prolactin associated with lactation may not have a noticeable effect on sexual desire. The majority (75%) of the 32 women in Kenny's (1973) study, for example, retrospectively reported no effect of the lactational period on sexual desire, and 78% of those who had weaned their children prior to assessment failed to recollect any change in desire after weaning (when prolactin levels had presumably returned to prelactation levels).

What effect, then, does prolactin have on sexual desire? We can glean no clear answer from the available studies, although the majority seem to indicate that prolactin itself may have little direct impact on desire. It is possible, however, that prolactin may influence desire indirectly, via an effect on mood or androgen production. Some researchers have hypothesized and provided evidence that prolactin secretion may provoke an increase or decrease in androgen levels (e.g., Eskin, Aspinall, & Segrave-Daly, 1985; Rubin, Gouin, Lubin, Poland, & Pirke, 1976). Low plasma testosterone levels have been noted in men with prolactin-secreting pituitary tumors (e.g., Faglia et al., 1977; Friesen, Tolis, Shiu, & Hwang, 1973), and hyperprolactinemia is frequently accompanied by low (in men) or high (in women) levels of plasma testosterone and other androgenic abnormalities (see Carter et al., 1978; Glickman, Rosenfield, Bergenstal, & Helke, 1982; Goodman, Molitch, Post, & Jackson, 1980; Legros, Chiodera, & Servalis, 1980; Schwartz et al., 1982). Insofar as androgens influence sexual interest, it is possible that the lowered desire seen in some hyperprolactinemic individuals may be due to the effect of elevated prolactin levels on androgen secretion.

Prolactin levels also may affect sexual desire indirectly through an influence on mood. Mild depression, anxiety, and hostility have been associated with high levels of prolactin (e.g., Buckman & Kellner, 1985; Fava, Fava, Kellner, Serafini, & Mastrogiacomo, 1981; Koppelman et al., 1987; but see Waterman et al., 1994), and hyperprolactinemic individuals with mood disturbances frequently return to normal mood during treatment with bromocriptine (Buckman & Kellner, 1985; Koppelman et al., 1987). As we will discuss in Chapter 5, evidence now suggests that mood (in particular, depressed mood) affects aspects of sexuality, including desire and interest; thus, it is possible that any decreases in sexual desire seen in hyperprolactinemic men and women are the result of mood alterations influenced by abnormally high prolactin secretion.

In sum, the role of prolactin in sexual desire remains unclear, despite numerous studies and substantial interest on the part of the scientific community.

* * *

It is probable that hormones influence sexual desire, although the precise nature of their role is unclear. In particular, there is strong empirical support for the notion that sexual desire in men and women requires certain minimal amounts of the androgens.

⅋ Hormonally Mediated Life Events

A second method of examining the relation between the sex hormones (e.g., androgens, estrogens, progesterone) and sexual desire involves investigating life events and changes that are hormonally mediated. The majority of major, hormonally mediated life events are exclusively female (e.g., menstruation, pregnancy, menopause). Women experience greater variations in circulating hormone levels during their lifetimes than do most men, and for this reason, women make ideal participants for researchers interested in the relationship between hormones and sexual desire. For the remainder of this chapter, then, we examine empirical research conducted to determine whether the hormonal fluctuations involved in three female life events—the menstrual cycle, pregnancy, and menopause—are reliably associated with rhythms, peaks, or changes in sexual desire.

The Menstrual Cycle

Most women menstruate and therefore experience rhythmic fluctuations in the primary sex hormones. One complete menstrual cycle generally ranges from 21 to 35 days in length, although the majority of women menstruate at approximately 28-day intervals (for a review of measurement techniques and phases of the menstrual cycle, see Regan, 1996a). A typical 28-day cycle profile is illustrated in Figure 3.1.

Some researchers have noted an association in women between the ovulatory portion of the menstrual cycle and increased sexual desire. The ovulatory phase generally occurs 14 days after the onset of the menses and is characterized by declining estrogen levels, rising progesterone levels, and relatively high amounts of the androgenic hormones. Specifically, a number of women have prospectively reported a significant increase or peak in sexual desire, feelings, fantasies, dreams, and free associations during this phase of the cycle (e.g., Adams, Gold, & Burt, 1978; Benedek & Rubenstein, 1939a, 1939b; Cavanagh, 1969; Harvey, 1987; Stanislaw & Rice, 1988). Although the techniques employed in many of these studies to estimate the timing of ovulation are diverse, the similarity in the above pattern of results is certainly worthy of note. In addition, at least one early study involving retrospective reports of sexual function has corroborated

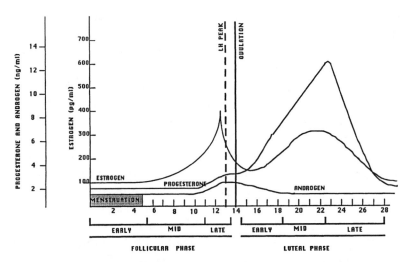

Figure 3.1. Hormonal Variations During the Menstrual Cycle
SOURCE: Adapted from Regan (1996a).
NOTE: Cycle days are labeled on the horizontal axis; mean values of estrogen, progesterone, and androgen are labeled on the vertical axis. This figure represents hormonal fluctuations during a typical cycle; not every woman will experience this precise pattern.

these findings. Cavanagh (1969) interviewed women who were currently using the rhythm method of contraception (which involves employing a mathematical formula to estimate fertile and nonfertile cycle phases); the majority indicated that their sexual desire was greatest at the time of ovulation.

This pattern is not universal, however. For example, several prospective studies have revealed an association between the mid-follicular phase or first postmenstrual week (characterized by low androgen and progesterone levels and rapidly rising estrogen levels) and peaks in sexual feelings, thoughts, and fantasies (Bancroft et al., 1983; Matteo & Rissman, 1984), and sexual interest and desire (Laessle, Tuschl, Schweiger, & Pirke, 1990; McCullough, 1974; Walker & Bancroft, 1990). In fact, even when different methods were employed to estimate the time of ovulation and standardize menstrual cycles of disparate length into one general pattern, Udry and Morris (1977) discovered that the desire for intercourse as reported in daily diaries tended to peak approximately 5 to 6 days prior to ovulation, during the mid-follicular phase. Similar results have been reported in retrospective studies; women in Warner and Bancroft's (1988) survey retrospectively reported experiencing mid-follicular highs in sexual interest. In direct opposition to the results noted above, then, these results indicate that desire, at least for some women, is more likely to peak during the first postmenstrual week.

Peaks in sexual desire also have been observed to occur during the late luteal period, commonly referred to as the premenstrual period. This phase of the menstrual cycle is associated with low androgen levels and rapidly falling progesterone and estrogen levels. Davis's (1926) sample retrospectively reported that their highest level of desire occurred on the 27th or 28th day of the cycle, just prior to menstruation, and more recently, Stewart's (1989) sample recalled an increase in sexual interest during this period. Similarly, 42% of the women in Chaturvedi and Chandra's (1990) study reported premenstrual increases in sexual desire, with 29% experiencing marked increases.

The studies cited above all found a single peak in desire, reported by women who experienced only one noticeable heightening or intensification of sexual feelings during the course of each menstrual cycle. Some women, however, experience more than one peak in sexual interest. Interestingly, the majority of those who report two reliable peaks in sexual desire each month also tend to do so during the ovulatory, mid-follicular, or late luteal phases, providing additional support for the hypothesis that all three of these phases are likely to be associated with peaks in desire and interest. For example, higher levels of sexual desire (Alexander, Sherwin, Bancroft, & Davidson, 1990) and sexual interest (Silber, 1994) have been prospectively reported by non-pill-using women during the postmenstrual (mid-follicular) and ovulatory phases. In addition, the majority of the 89 women in an early study conducted by Davis (1926) who experienced two periods of heightened sexual desire each month retrospectively reported that these occurred on Days 5 to 8 of the cycle, during the mid-follicular phase, and also on cycle Days 26 to 28, or the late luteal phase. Of Tinklepaugh's (1933) sample, 44% experienced a similar bimodal rhythm of sexual desire, prospectively reporting immediate pre- and postmenstrual peaks (again, during what we have respectively termed the late luteal and mid-follicular phases), and McCance, Luff, and Widdowson's (1937) analysis of daily log data revealed that women experienced a primary peak in sexual feeling on cycle Day 8, as well as a secondary, lesser peak on the 26th cycle day. Similar results are reported by Hart (1960), who assessed "interest in having inter-course," and by Ferrero and La Pietra (1971), who measured "libido."

Thus, it appears that sexual desire, in general, reaches its peak intensity or greatest frequency during the mid-follicular phase, char-acterized by low androgen and progesterone levels and rapidly rising estrogen levels; and/or around ovulation, a time of relatively high androgen levels, rising progesterone levels, and rapidly descending estrogen levels; and/or during the late luteal phase, associated with low androgen levels and rapidly falling progesterone and estrogen levels. However, although some agreement appears to exist as to the timing of such peaks in sexual desire, the assumption that such peaks occur in all women is unwarranted. Desire may peak once or twice in any given menstrual cycle, but it may also occur fairly consistently throughout the course of the entire cycle and thus fail to reach a noticeable peak. For example, approximately 34.4% of Ferrero and La Pietra's (1971) sample, 34% of Hart's (1960) sample, and 29.5% of Davis's (1926) sample failed to observe or report any periodicity of sexual desire or feelings. For these women, desire may be high or low or even moderate; whatever the case, this aspect of sexual experience appears to progress along on a relatively even keel, untouched by soaring highs or precipitous lows.

Conclusion. Sexual desire does appear to increase during certain menstrual cycle phases for some women. Specifically, the subset of women who experience one single peak in desire tend to do so at ovulation or during the weeks immediately prior to or subsequent to menstruation. Those women who experience more than one peak in desire also tend to do so during two of the aforementioned phases (i.e., ovulation, mid-follicular, late luteal). Other women, however, do not report reliable peaks or fluctuations in their feelings of sexual interest and desire. Consequently, no single rhythmic pattern emerges that can be said to definitively characterize the sexual experience of the human female.

Pregnancy

A variety of research now indicates that pregnancy, with its progressive increase in progesterone, estradiol, and estriol levels, is characterized by a more or less progressive *decrease* in sexual desire. Women asked to report retrospectively on their sexual experiences during the first trimester of pregnancy generally recall either no change or a decline from prepregnancy levels in sexual interest (e.g., Perkins, 1979; Solberg, Butler, & Wagner, 1973) and sexual desire (e.g., Kenny, 1973; Ryding, 1984). Similar results have been obtained from prospective studies; the majority of women report either no change or a decrease from prepregnancy levels in aspects of sexual experience such as "sex drive" (e.g., Robson, Brant, & Kumar, 1981), sexual desire (e.g., Falicov, 1973; Lumley, 1978), and desire for intercourse or sexual activity (e.g., Reamy, White, Daniell, & Le Vine, 1982; Tolor & DiGrazia, 1976). During the second trimester, many women continue to retrospectively report either no change in sexual desire from prepregnancy levels (e.g., Kenny, 1973; Ryding, 1984) or less sexual interest than during the first trimester (e.g., Holtzman, 1976; Perkins, 1979; Solberg et al., 1973). Prospectively, the majority report decreased sexual desire (e.g., Falicov, 1973; Lumley, 1978; Tolor & DiGrazia, 1976); however, for some women, sexual desire is greater than that reported for the first trimester, although still less than prepregnancy levels (e.g., Reamy et al., 1982). Both retrospectively and prospectively, women report experiencing the greatest decline in sexual interest and desire for intercourse or sexual activity during the last few months of pregnancy, particularly as delivery draws increasingly nearer (e.g., Falicov, 1973; Holtzman, 1976; Kenny, 1973; Lumley, 1978; Perkins, 1979; Reamy et al., 1982; Ryding, 1984; Solberg et al., 1973; Tolor & DiGrazia, 1976).

Menopause

The term *perimenopause* or *climacteric* refers to a transitional period of declining female reproductive capacity and ovarian function that encompasses the menopause, or final menstrual flow. *Postmenopause* refers to the entire period of life following the final menstrual flow (e.g., Gosden, 1985). The primary endocrinologic events of perimenopause are decreased total ovarian production of estrogens and the eventual cessation of cyclic estradiol secretion, as well as decreased concentrations of androgens, progesterone, and prolactin (e.g., Benjamin & Seltzer, 1987).

Some empirical data support an association between menopause and a decline in sexual desire or interest. Women monitored throughout perimenopause, for example, report experiencing significantly fewer sexual thoughts and fantasies than prior to the last menstrual period (e.g., McCoy & Davidson, 1985), and also retrospectively report less desire for intercourse since the menopause (e.g., Channon & Ballinger, 1986). However, the diminution of desire reported by the some of these women may be accounted for at least in part by the various vaginal changes and symptoms associated with decreased estrogen levels. For example, McCoy and Davidson (1985) found that postmenopausal women who prospectively indicated experiencing fewer sexual thoughts or fantasies than they had prior to menopause also suffered more from lack of vaginal lubrication during intercourse. Similarly, women who retrospectively reported a decrease in sexual desire since entering perimenopause (Channon & Ballinger, 1986) were also significantly more likely to suffer from vaginal dryness and to experience pain during intercourse. In view of these findings, it seems plausible to suggest that what at least some peri- and postmenopausal women experience is not a lack of desire for sexual activity per se but, rather, a lack of interest in uncomfortable sexual activity. (Indeed, Mansfield, Voda, and Koch, 1995, found that vaginal dryness was associated with decreased sexual desire in [not necessarily perimenopausal] 35-55 year-old women.)

Studies conducted by other researchers also challenge the notion that perimenopausal and postmenopausal women inevitably experience less sexual desire than their younger, more hormonally viable counterparts. Persky et al. (1982) discovered that although the mean adrenal androgen levels (determined by analysis of blood samples) of younger, menstruating women were significantly higher than those obtained for older, fully postmenopausal women, both groups reported the same levels of sexual desire at the time of assessment.

Hormonal changes obviously do occur with the onset of menopause, but this study, at least, indicates that such changes do not necessarily affect the experience of sexual desire. More recently, Cutler, Garcia, and McCoy (1987) assessed dimensions of sexual desire in a group of 124 perimenopausal women via questions about, among other things, the frequency of and recent changes in sexual fantasy. Less than 10% of the sample retrospectively noticed a change in the frequency of sexual fantasy that they felt was related to menopausal changes. A prospective, 11-year longitudinal study conducted by Koster and Garde (1993) similarly found no relationship between self-reported sexual desire and menopausal status in a large group of 51-year-old women. These results certainly support the hypothesis that the capacity for and experience of sexual desire may not be dramatically altered by the onset of ovarian decline.

In sum, it is difficult to know what effect the decrease in estrogens and other sex hormones associated with the menopause has on sexual desire; however, most studies seem to suggest that this hormonally mediated life event does not necessarily result in decreased sexual desire in women.

❧ Conclusions

The subjective experience of sexual desire clearly is related, at least in part, to the levels of circulating hormones in our bodies. In particular, the androgenic hormones appear to be most closely linked to this human life experience. However, hormones alone do not determine whether an individual will or will not feel sexual desire. In the next chapter, we examine other important internal or intraindividual correlates of sexual desire.

4

Sexual Desire
The Body (Part II)

As was apparent from the last chapter, hormonal processes have been the subject of much investigation by researchers interested in determining the causes and correlates of sexual desire. Other, perhaps no less important, internal factors have not received as much attention. We conclude our examination of the "body" of desire by considering physical health, age, sex or gender, and drug use.

◆ Physical Health

The association between physical health and sexual desire has only recently been examined. However, questionnaire and interview studies consistently demonstrate an association between serious physical illness or disability and chronically or temporarily decreased sexual desire. For example, in a study conducted by Schreiner-Engel, Schiavi, Vietorisz, Eichel, and Smith (1985), diabetic women and a matched control group of women completed the Derogatis Sexual Functioning Inventory (DSFI) and participated in a semistructured interview about sexual experiences. The DSFI profiles of both groups were largely within the normal range; however, the diabetic women scored significantly lower than did the nondiabetic women on the subscale designed to assess "sexual drive." Interview data corroborated this finding; diabetic women reported having less desire for sexual intercourse than nondiabetics (see also Schreiner-Engel, Schiavi, Vietorisz, & Smith, 1987). Similarly, men and women with cancer report experiencing decreased sexual desire after treatment (e.g., Schover, Evans, & von Eschenbach, 1987), and 44% of the men and 71% of the women with Parkinson's disease in Koller et al.'s (1990) study stated that their sexual interest was less than before they had the disease (and a decrease in the Parkinsonian person's sexual interest was noted by the spouse in 54% of the cases). The excessive weight loss associated with anorexia nervosa may also inhibit sexual desire. Of the 31 anorexic women interviewed by Beumont, Abraham, and Simson (1981), 81% reported that their "libido" and "sexual interest" had definitely decreased following weight loss (for additional discussion of anorexia and sexual function see de Silva, 1993).

Conversely, a return to relatively good physical health may be accompanied by an increase in sexual desire. Schover, Novick, Steinmuller, and Goormastic (1990) reported that men and women with end-stage renal disease experienced a marked increase in sexual desire after renal transplantation; specifically, these researchers asked men and women to compare their feelings of sexual desire during the 6 months preceding transplant surgery with their sexual desire during the 6 months immediately following the transplant. The median frequency of men's sexual desire changed from once per week before surgery to twice a week after surgery, and women's median desire increased from once a month to once a week.

In sum, research on sexual desire and physical health points to the (perhaps commonsensical) conclusion that we are more likely to be interested in sexual experiences when we feel physically "good" than when we do not.

❧ Age

A variety of beliefs and misconceptions exist with respect to sexuality and age. If the puberty-stricken teenager is assumed in Western society to be a quivering mass of sexual desire, then the preadolescent and the elderly are portrayed as asexual beings with little interest in or capacity for sexual experience. Although people undergo a series of physical changes with the onset of puberty (and also with aging) that may affect the capacity for sexual desire, the lack of research on sexual desire in children or adolescents precludes any firm conclusions about the course of sexual desire during the early years of life. However, cross-sectional research on aging men and women consistently demonstrates a decline in sexual desire or interest with advancing age, as well as considerable variability within age groups (e.g., Antonovsky, Sadowsky, & Maoz, 1990; Hallstrom, 1979; Lunde, Larsen, Fog, & Garde, 1991; Mulligan & Moss, 1991; Pfeiffer, Verwoerdt, & Davis, 1972). Schiavi, Schreiner-Engel, Mandeli, Schanzer, and Cohen (1990), for example, interviewed 65 healthy married men between the ages of 45 and 74 years and reported that participants' responses to three self-report measures of sexual desire (i.e., frequency of desire for sex, frequency of sexual thoughts, and maximum amount of time comfortable without sex) were significantly negatively correlated with age. Similarly, Purifoy, Grodsky, and Giambra (1992) examined the association between age and sexual desire in a cross-sectional sample of women aged 26 to 78 years. Participants' self-reported "desire for sex" and desired frequency of "sexual relations with a partner" were both significantly negatively correlated with age; conversely, the estimated length of time that participants believed they "could comfortably go without sexual activity of any kind" (also defined for participants as the upper limit of time when they would "be very much aware of sexual need") was positively correlated with age.

Very few longitudinal studies to date have assessed changes in sexual desire over the life span. Hallstrom and Samuelsson (1990) asked a sample of 497 women who ranged in age from 38 to 54 years of age to indicate whether their present degree of sexual desire was strong, moderate, weak, or lacking and then asked them to respond to the same question 6 years later. Ninety-nine (29%) of the 345 women who reported experiencing strong or moderate sexual desire at the first interview reported a lower level of desire at the time of the second interview; and more specifically, 14 of the 15 women (93%) who initially reported a strong sexual desire reported lower levels at the 6-year follow-up interview. Other longitudinal studies find contradictory results. Koster and Garde (1993), for example, surveyed a sample of 474 women at the ages of 40, 45, and 51 about their frequency of sexual desire and reported that sexual desire remained largely stable over time (with 70% of the women experiencing no change in sexual desire during this 11-year period).

In sum, it appears that sexual desire is more likely to decrease or remain stable, rather than to increase, with age. However, the prevalence of cross-sectional studies and potential cohort effects make it difficult to interpret these findings. In addition, pervasive stereotypes exist that depict older people as having little interest in sex, as sexually unattractive, and as unable to perform sexually (e.g., Butler & Lewis, 1976, 1986; Levy, 1994). These popular myths, coupled with strong social norms that suggest that sexual desire is the prerogative of youth and therefore is inappropriate when experienced by older individuals, may influence participants' ability and motivation to recall and report their feelings of sexual desire. Clearly, more research is needed in this area.

⟐ Sex and Gender

When discussing the sexual life of men and women, Krafft-Ebing (1886/1945) states, "Man has beyond doubt the stronger sexual appetite of the two" (p. 14). The notion that men have stronger and more frequent sexual desires than women has been a pervasive theme in contemporary Western culture, and some research does suggest that sex differences exist with respect to perceptions of the sexual desire of others, prevalence of sexual desire disorders, and self-reported amount of sexual desire experienced. For example, several studies indicate that men perceive people to be more interested in sex than do women. Zellman and Goodchilds (1983) asked adolescent boys and girls to rate the extent to which a variety of cues (e.g., revealing clothing) in a dating situation indicated a desire to have sex. They found that boys in general perceived cues as indicating more sexual intent than did girls. Men also may impute more sexual meaning to heterosexual interactions than do women. Abbey (1982) conducted a laboratory experiment in which male-female dyads were instructed to interact with each other for 5 minutes while a second, hidden male-female dyad observed this interaction. She found that male observers (and actors) rated female actors as more "seductive" and "promiscuous" than did females, and male actors and observers reported greater "sexual attraction" to the opposite-sex actor than did female actors and observers. Not only were men inclined to rate the female actor in sexual terms, but they also rated the male actor in a similar manner; male actors perceived themselves as more "seductive" than female actors perceived them, and male actors perceived themselves (and male observers perceived them) as more "promiscuous" than females did. Another study conducted by Abbey and Melby (1986) corroborated these findings. Men and women rated photographs of a male-female dyad seated at a table studying; regardless of the amount of interpersonal distance between the target couple, men rated both the male and female stimulus person as being significantly more sexy, seductive, and promiscuous than did women (also see Shotland & Craig, 1988). Women are also more likely than men to report having had their friendliness toward someone of the opposite sex mistakenly perceived as a sign of sexual attraction or interest (e.g., Abbey, 1987).

Not only do men appear to perceive more sexual interest on the part of others and themselves than do women, but some clinical interviews and surveys report a higher frequency of sexual desire disorders (i.e., low or hypoactive sexual desire) in women than men. For example, Segraves and Segraves (1991) recruited 906 men and women for a study of sexual disorders. Of the 588 people with a diagnosis of hypoactive sexual desire disorder, 475 (81%) were women. However, the number of men with sexual desire problems appears to be on the rise. According to LoPiccolo and Friedman (1988), 70% of the clinical cases of low sexual desire from 1974 to 1976 were women, but this percentage decreased to 60% between 1977 and 1978; and the percentage of men with low sexual desire increased from 40% of the cases during 1977 and 1978 to 55% of the cases during 1982 and 1983 (also see Mohl & Pedersen, 1991). Some authors suggest that the rising number of cases of low or hypoactive sexual desire, seen mainly in men, may result in part from changing social mores that deem it more acceptable for women to expect a satisfying and active sexual relationship and to express their own sexual desire to their partner. This increased freedom of sexual expression in turn may increase the likelihood that a lack of male desire or interest will be noticed and labeled as a "problem" by both partners.

Although the clinical literature suggests that women are more likely than men to experience low levels of sexual desire, few researchers have investigated the self-reported amount of sexual desire experienced by men and women in nonclinical samples. However, a survey of Colombian high school students conducted by Useche, Villegas, and Alzate (1990) revealed that a significantly higher percentage of young men (80.2%) than young women (48.5%) reported experiencing sexual desire at least once a week. Similar results were reported by Beck et al. (1991). These researchers asked undergraduate men and women to answer the question, "How often do you experience sexual desire," with eight response options that ranged from "never" to "several times a day." Although no men and only 2.3% of the women stated that they never experienced sexual desire, significantly more men (94.6%) than women (72.2%) reported experiencing sexual desire at least once per week.

Other research, however, suggests that women are as likely as men to experience sexual desire and other subjective sexual events. For example, similar numbers of men (94%) and women (95%) surveyed by Davidson (1985) indicated that they had experienced a sexual fantasy. In addition, a recent study by Sprecher and Regan (1996) reveals that college-aged men and women virgins do not abstain from sexual intercourse due to lack of sexual desire. The least important reason for virginity given by both men and women was "I lack desire for sex." Apparently, both men and women desired sex but abstained from it due to other reasons (such as not having met the "right" sexual partner, wishing to avoid pregnancy and disease, and acting in the service of personal beliefs). This finding certainly argues against the notion that men have more frequent desires than do women.

It is possible that men in fact are more sexually interested than women. However, some researchers suggest that purported sex differences in desire stem from the greater willingness of men to report sexual feelings on a self-report instrument (e.g., Metts, Sprecher, & Regan, 1998). In addition, women may be less likely than men to interpret or label particular experiences or feelings as sexual desire. For example, in an early study of sexual desire and the menstrual cycle, Cavanagh (1969) found it necessary to teach his women participants how to recognize sexual desire and how to make the connection between that term and specific subjective sexual feelings they could expect to experience. In sum, then, it appears that men are more likely to perceive sexual desire on the part of others; however, the evidence remains mixed with respect to sex differences in actual frequency of sexual desire. The intensity (as opposed to the frequency) of sexual desire experienced by men and women has yet to be systematically investigated.

❧ Drugs

Folk wisdom suggests that some substances function as aphrodisiacs that trigger or enhance sexual desire. The number of putative aphrodisiacs is legion. Artichokes, celery, tomatoes, truffles, and garlic, for example, have been imbued with amatory properties (e.g., Connell, 1965; Edwards, 1971; Wedeck, 1961). In addition to herbs and foodstuffs, many of the so-called recreational drugs are commonly believed to enhance sexual desire. A specific drug may have different effects depending on both the amount used and the duration of use, and thus it is necessary to distinguish between the acute and chronic effects of drug use. The former concerns the impact of small, moderate, or excessive single doses on sexual functioning, whereas chronic effects refer to the impact of extended, high-dose usage. For reviews of the relation between drug use and other sexual experiences (e.g., sexual arousal, orgasm), readers are referred to Buffum (1982) and Buffum, Moser, and Smith (1988). For reviews of the effects of drugs developed and used primarily for medical purposes (e.g., hypertensives, antipsychotics, antidepressants) on sexual function, readers are referred to Crenshaw and Goldberg (1996); Money, Leal, and Gonzalez-Heydrich (1988); and Sitsen (1988).

Depressants

In small to moderate doses, some central nervous system depressants (e.g., methaqualone) induce sleep, whereas others—such as alcohol and barbiturates—may produce physiologically and psychologically stimulating effects such as increased heart and respiration rates, vasodilation, feelings of anxiety, energy, exhilaration, and talkative, euphoric behavior. Higher doses of depressants may result in anxiety, depression, mood shifts, restlessness and irritability, unsteady gait, slurred speech, delirium, and poor judgment (e.g., Berry & Brain, 1986; Harvey, 1985; Wesson & Smith, 1981), all effects not likely to be conducive to the experience of sexual desire.

Alcohol. Alcohol has long been prized as an aphrodisiac; King Louis XIV is reputed to have used alcohol sweetened with sugar to promote his "amorous feelings" (Wedeck, 1961), and many recreational drug users also believe that alcohol provokes sexual desire, at least in small to moderate amounts. For example, Harvey and Beckman (1986) asked 69 nonalcoholic women about their experiences with alcohol and sex. The majority (61.2%) of the women retrospectively reported desiring sexual activity most when drinking (i.e., under the influence of alcohol) compared with when not drinking. In addition, more of these social drinkers associated increased sexual desire with drinking a little (44.8%) than with drinking a lot (16.4%). They also asked the women in their sample to keep daily logs monitoring their alcohol consumption and sexual experiences for an average period of 3 months. Analysis of these daily logs revealed that "sexual drive"—defined by the researchers as sexual desire, fantasy, masturbation, female- and mutually initiated sexual activities, and female sexual advances rejected by the partner—was *negatively* correlated with alcohol consumption. Specifically, mean scores on the sexual drive index were significantly higher following *no* alcohol consumption than following moderate (three or fewer drinks) or heavy (more than three drinks) ingestion of alcohol. Thus, although the participants recalled greater desire while drinking, they actually experienced the opposite.

Chronic ingestion of alcohol also has been linked with decreased sexual desire. Although the correlational studies that characterize this research do not permit inferences about causality, some surveys find a higher incidence of reduced sexual desire in men and women alcoholics than in nonalcoholics. For example, Heiser and Hartmann (1987) administered a questionnaire to a sample of 55 women alcoholics and a matched sample of 54 nonalcoholics. The results of this survey indicated that significantly more alcoholic women than controls stated that their sexual desire had decreased during the course of their lifetimes, with 6% of the alcoholics reporting that they had never been "in the mood" for sexual encounters and none of the control group making such a report.

Barbiturates. No experimental and few correlational studies have been conducted on the effects of barbituric acid derivatives (i.e., pentobarbital, secobarbital, amobarbital, and butabarbital) on sexual function, although some evidence suggests that low doses of barbiturates, like alcohol, may be associated with enhanced likelihood of sexual desire. For example, one of the drug users in a survey conducted by Gay, Newmeyer, Perry, Johnson, and Kurland (1982) claimed that "downers just plain make you want to get it on—with *anyone*" (p. 116). However, the majority of users, as well as researchers who have investigated the question, conclude that barbiturate use is more likely to be related to diminished sexual desire, sexual interest, sexual appetite, or libido, particularly at high single doses (e.g., Edwards, 1971; Ellinwood & Rockwell, 1975; Gay, Newmeyer, Elion, & Wieder, 1975; Gay & Sheppard, 1972; Kaplan, 1979; Winick, 1981). The effects of chronic excessive use of barbiturates are unknown, although some researchers speculate that barbiturate dependency is associated with a decrease in sexual desire (e.g., Ellinwood & Rockwell, 1975).

Methaqualone. Some methaqualone users believe that this drug is endowed with aphrodisiac properties. Gerald and Schwirian (1973) surveyed 66 men and women methaqualone users whose average duration of use was 1 year and who confined themselves to roughly 1 to 4 instances of use each month. The majority (77%) of these respondents *expected* methaqualone to make them "want to make love," and 42% expected it to "increase [their] sexual desires or breakdown [the] sexual resistance of others." In addition, 97% and 95%, respectively, reported actually experiencing these effects after using methaqualone. However, some researchers believe that methaqualone, if it has any effect at all apart from the psychological effects of expectation, is more likely to result in decreased sexual desire, particularly at high single doses or with chronic use (e.g., Gay et al., 1975; Gay & Sheppard, 1972).

Stimulants

Amphetamine and cocaine are central nervous system stimulants that in small to moderate doses may result in mood elevation, a sense of well-being and energy, self-confidence, increased psychomotor activity, elevated blood pressure, and appetite suppression. At higher doses, individuals may also experience headache, nausea, delirium, anxiety, tremors and convulsions, and hallucinations. Chronic stimulant use causes symptoms similar to acute overdosage but more frequently includes insomnia, fatigue, depression, marked weight loss, and psychotic reactions with hallucinations and paranoid delusions (e.g., Clark, 1952; Kramer, 1972; Morgan, 1981; Van Dyke, 1981; Washton, Gold, & Pottash, 1984).

Amphetamine. Although amphetamine is a unique chemical, the term *amphetamine* commonly is used to refer to stimulant drugs of the amphetamine type or to amphetamine and closely related chemical compounds. Some researchers hypothesize that enhanced sexual desire may be experienced at low to moderate doses but impaired at higher doses (e.g., Kaplan, 1979; Smith, Buxton, & Dammann, 1979; Winick, 1981); however, the empirical evidence pertaining to amphetamine's acute effects is not conclusive. In P. Connell's (1958) sample, for example, the percentage of amphetamine users who reported increased libido, defined by the author as "sexual drive," when high on amphetamine (25%) was matched by those who said that it decreased their sexual drive. Bell and Trethowan (1961) presented several case studies in which addicts variously reported both increased and decreased "sexual drive" after high single doses of amphetamine. It may be that the initial effect of moderate to high doses is one of heightened sexual desire that then diminishes when the drug's effects begin to wear off. Indeed, 30 of 36 men and women patients interviewed by Gay and Sheppard (1972) at a detoxification clinic stated that high doses of amphetamine greatly augmented their sexual drive and the desire for sexual activity but that diminished sexual interest occurred toward the end of a several-day "run." No empirical evidence exists with respect to chronic amphetamine use and sexual desire, but researchers generally assume that chronic use is associated with decreased sexual desire (e.g., Kaplan, 1979; Winick, 1981; but see Connell, 1958).

Cocaine. Cocaine was popularized in the Western world by Sigmund Freud, who wrote of its stimulant properties and advocated its use as an aphrodisiac (e.g., 1884/1963b). Although empirical evidence is largely nonexistent, many researchers conclude that cocaine, like amphetamine, may be associated with increased sexual desire in small to moderate doses and with diminished or lost sexual desire in high single and/or frequent doses (e.g., Clark, 1952; Hofmann, 1983; Hollister, 1975; Kaplan, 1979; Money et al., 1988; Washton et al., 1984; Winick, 1981). Indeed, cocaine has been touted by users for its sexual desire-enhancing ability; for example, a sample of 100 men and women drug users surveyed by Gay et al. (1975) ranked cocaine first over a variety of other substances in terms of its ability to increase sexual desire.

Opiates

Opiates (i.e., opium, morphine, heroin) are derived from the opium poppy and synthetic manufacture and have been used medicinally to relieve pain, anxiety, coughing, and diarrhea. After opiate ingestion or injection, individuals experience mood changes, euphoria, drowsiness, loss of anxiety, slurred speech, unsteady gait, decreased pulse and respiration rates, constipation, and sometimes nausea and dizziness; more extreme reactions, including pronounced respiratory depression, are found at higher doses (e.g., Deneau & Mule, 1981; Hofmann, 1983; Jaffe & Martin, 1985).

Opium and Morphine. Although there is a paucity of correlational evidence—and no experimental data—on the acute effects of opium and morphine on sexual desire, some research suggests that they may be associated with a lack of sexual desire. Douglas (1931) anecdotally related that ingestion of a small dose of opium mainly resulted, in his personal experience, in nonerotic, blissful dreams, and other clinicians and researchers argue in their reviews of the drug literature that single high doses may diminish sexual desire in both men and women (e.g., Deneau & Mule, 1981; Edwards, 1971; Kaplan, 1979). Even less is known about the effects of chronic use of these drugs, but Wikler (1952) reported a case study of an opium addict who currently evinced "no desire for sexual intercourse" (p. 276).

Heroin and Methadone. Heroin users often retrospectively report diminished sexual desire while under the influence of this synthetic morphine derivative. For example, 41% of a sample of 95 male and female drug users surveyed by Gay et al. (1975) stated that heroin made them "lose interest in sex." Cushman (1972) reported that 92% of his sample of 13 former addicts who claimed that their libido (defined by the author as "sexual desires") was presently normal reported impaired or absent libido "when high on heroin," and Gay and Sheppard (1972) noted that individual users recalled that sexual interest reappeared during the time that they were "coming off" a heroin-induced high. Chronic use of heroin also may be associated with little desire for or interest in sexual activities (e.g., Cushman, 1972; Mendelson & Mello, 1982). De Leon and Wexler (1973) asked 31 male heroin addicts, currently drug free and residing in a therapeutic community, to estimate their general level of sexual desire during the preaddiction, addiction, and postaddiction periods. The majority (84%) retrospectively reported a decrease in sexual desire from the preaddiction to the addiction period, and 87% noted an increase in sexual desire from the addiction to the current, postaddiction period.

Methadone is a synthetic analgesic, pharmacologically similar to morphine, used as a heroin substitute. Some researchers believe that methadone use is associated with increased sexual desire in former heroin addicts, but not over and above preaddiction levels (e.g., Ellinwood & Rockwell, 1975; Winick, 1981). However, a series of interviews conducted by Hanbury, Cohen, and Stimmel (1977) revealed that 38% of 17 male heroin addicts enrolled in a methadone maintenance and aftercare treatment program retrospectively reported a lack of "sexual drive" during the periods when they were on methadone maintenance and on heroin, whereas none reported a lack of sexual drive during the drug-free period. In general, then, methadone does not appear to have aphrodisiac properties, either in acute single doses or after chronic ingestion.

Hallucinogens

Also known as psychedelics, hallucinogens are a group of drugs that alter conscious experience. Lysergic acid diethylamide (LSD) is the most powerful member of this class of drugs, whose other members include 3,4-Methylenedioxyamphetamine (MDA), 3,4-Methylenedioxymethyl-amphetamine (MDMA), phencyclidine (PCP), and mescaline. Low to moderate doses of hallucinogenic drugs result in sensory, visual, and temporal distortions; feelings of depersonalization; delusions; impaired performance on tests involving concentration, attention, and motivation; slurred speech and unsteady gait; elevated blood pressure; and sometimes depression, anxiety, confusion, and agitation. Terrified reactions to hallucinations may occur at higher doses, and chronic users may experience depression, paranoia, psychoses, and flashbacks to previous drug-induced states (e.g., Ungerleider & De Angelis, 1981). None of the hallucinogenic drugs has any currently acceptable medical use, and little is known about their impact on sexual desire. For example, although Hollister (1975) argued that the amphetamine-like effects of these substances may contribute to an increase in "sexual interest" (p. 89), Weil (1976) suggested that MDA tends to "decrease the desire for orgasm" and any "hunger for sex" (p. 336). Similarly, although Gay et al. (1975) concluded that LSD ingestion is associated with increased sexual desire, several of their respondents stated that the drug makes them lose interest in sex, and only 4 of 49 men and women (8.2%) interviewed at a detoxification clinic in an earlier study reported increased "sex desire" with LSD (Gay & Sheppard, 1972).

Marijuana

Known as *marijuana, ganja, pot, grass,* or *weed,* the dried leaves of the hemp plant (*Cannabis sativa*) contain the psychoactive compound delta-9-tetrahydrocannabinol (THC). When smoked or ingested, small to moderate doses of marijuana may result in increased sensitivity to sound, distorted time sense, increased heart rate, anxiety, and sedation, whereas the consumption of heavier doses results in decreased heart rate and sometimes an acute anxiety episode or the reexperience of any previous LSD flashbacks. Chronic heavy users experience lethargy, muscle tension and soreness, nausea, decreased coordination, slow speech, coughing, and bronchitis (e.g., Grinspoon & Bakalar, 1981; Hofmann, 1983).

Drug users frequently assume that marijuana use is associated with increased sexual desire. For example, roughly 44% of the 97 men and women surveyed by Halikas, Weller, and Morse (1982) reported that marijuana acts as an "aphrodisiac," although only 9% felt that the effect was strong. The men and women drug users surveyed by Gay et al. (1975) believed marijuana to be second only to cocaine in terms of its ability to increase sexual desire. However, clinicians and researchers believe that marijuana has little or variable acute effects on sexual desire (e.g., Edwards, 1971; Grinspoon & Bakalar, 1981; Kaplan, 1979; Winick, 1981), and little is known about the impact of its chronic use.

Conclusion

None of the drugs reviewed above appears to have a consistent impact on sexual desire; hence, none can be said to function as a true aphrodisiac (or, alternatively, as an antiaphrodisiac). However, research does suggest that enhanced sexual desire may be related to the use of small to moderate amounts of alcohol and the stimulants (e.g., cocaine, amphetamine, and related chemicals). Moderate doses of opium and heroin appear to be associated with decreased sexual desire, and lower doses of methaqualone, barbiturates, and marijuana appear to have mixed effects on sexual desire. The impact of methadone and the hallucinogens remains unclear. Diminished sexual desire is generally associated with heavier doses of depressants, opiates, and cocaine; the effects of excessive single doses of amphetamine, its derivatives, and hallucinogenic drugs are unknown. Chronic use of alcohol, heroin, and the stimulant drugs is associated with reduced or lost sexual desire. No firm conclusions can be drawn about the effects of chronic use of barbiturates, methaqualone, hallucinogens, opium, and marijuana, although to the extent that such chronic usage is generally debilitating, both physically and psychologically, the capacity to experience sexual desire also is likely to be impaired.

It is difficult to interpret the available research on the association between drug ingestion and sexual desire for many reasons. For example, some drugs, particularly the depressants, are effective at relieving tension and social inhibitions at lower doses. Indeed, recreational drug users frequently report feeling more relaxed in sexual situations when under the influence of alcohol (e.g., Klassen & Wilsnack, 1986). Thus, these drugs may not directly increase desire but, rather, may relieve anxieties associated with sexual activity. Another reason, discussed below, is that the psychological effect of expectation that a drug will increase sexual desire and enjoyment of sexual activities has rarely been experimentally separated out from the physical action of the drug. Finally, a variety of interpersonal, psychological, and physiological conditions may render the chronic user susceptible to reduced sexual desire. For example, alcoholic relationships are often dysfunctional (e.g., Schiavi, 1990), alcoholics frequently report depression and anxiety (e.g., Goodwin, 1976), and chronic abuse of alcohol, heroin, or marijuana has adverse effects on virtually all major body organs (e.g., Berry & Brain, 1986) and also may result in decreased levels of sex hormones (e.g., Mendelson & Mello, 1982; Van Thiel, Gavaler, & Tarter, 1988). All of these factors may impair the ability to experience sexual desire and thus may account for the diminished sexual interest reported by chronic drug users.

In sum, it is possible that drug ingestion, particularly when excessive and chronic, plays a role in determining or altering the experience of sexual desire. However, the scarcity of experimental studies in this area and the abundance of alternative explanations for the correlational findings makes it difficult to delineate this role.

❧ Conclusions: The Role of Psychological Expectations and Placebo Effects

As we will discuss in the next chapter, the impact of psychological expectation on sexual desire only recently has been examined. However, at least one study suggests that the increased sexual desire experienced at low to moderate doses of alcohol and other drugs may result from beliefs and expectations about their effects on sexual function rather than from drug ingestion per se. Barling and Fincham

(1980) conducted an elegant experimental study in which nonalcoholic men were randomly assigned to a "no-alcohol control group," a "simulated alcohol group" in which they received no alcohol but were asked to complete the experimental measures as if they had consumed a fairly large quantity of alcohol, a "placebo group" who received soda in a whisky-besmeared cup, a ".4 gram alcohol group" who received .4 grams of alcohol per kilogram of body weight, and a ".8 gram alcohol group" who received .8 grams per kilogram body weight. Five weeks prior to participation and immediately following the experimental manipulation, the men completed a sexual experience questionnaire that contained items covering a wide range of sexual behavior (e.g., held hands with someone of the opposite sex, deep-kissed with someone of the opposite sex, and so on). Participants rated each item on a variety of measures, including an indicant of sexual interest (i.e., "have not done but would like to"). The researchers found significant group differences on the sexual interest variable such that the .8 alcohol group demonstrated a significantly higher pretest-posttest difference from all the other groups. More important, this significant result disappeared when the researchers controlled for men's estimation of the alcohol content of their drink; that is, with beliefs about alcohol content controlled statistically, the increase in self-report of desired sexual experiences (an indication of sexual interest) seen at the higher dose of alcohol disappeared. Therefore, it appears possible that the enhanced sexual desire reported by some drug users simply may represent a self-fulfilling prophecy of their beliefs and expectations about the drug's effects rather than any inherent aphrodisiac quality of the drug itself. Expectation thus may play an important role in determining sexual desire. This is the question to which we turn in the following chapter. Specifically, we move away from the "body" and focus instead on the "mind" of desire—on the impact of beliefs, assumptions, expectations, moods, and emotions.

5

Sexual Desire
The Mind

The last two chapters explored the variety of physical factors that contribute to and shape the experience of sexual desire. In this chapter, we focus on the "mind" of desire—the mental, emotional, and psychological antecedents and correlates of sexual desire. First, we examine the ways in which affective expectations and sociocultural norms—beliefs about what one should and will feel in a given situation with a particular person—may influence the experience and expression of sexual desire. We also consider the specific beliefs that men and women have about the nature and causes of sexual desire, a topic that only now is beginning to receive empirical attention. We end by reviewing research on the association between sexual desire and personality, past experiences, and mood and emotion.

⚬ Affective Expectations
About Sexual Desire

The impact of affective expectations on actual reactions, a heretofore neglected area of inquiry, has been the focus of relatively recent
theoretical and empirical attention (e.g., Kirsch, 1990; Wilson & Klaaren,
1992; Wilson, Lisle, Kraft, & Wetzel, 1989). Affective expectations are
defined by Wilson and Klaaren (1992) as "people's predictions about
how they will feel in a particular situation or toward a specific
stimulus" (p. 3). As observed by these researchers, people undoubtedly have affective expectations about the type and amount of emotion they will experience in a given situation or for a given target.

It seems probable that people possess expectations about sexual desire
as well and that such expectations may determine whether or not they
actually experience sexual desire. These expectations may derive from
previous reactions to a stimulus (i.e., target-based expectancies; Jones
& McGillis, 1976), as when a man expects to feel sexual desire while
sitting in a darkened movie theater cuddling with his beloved because
he has always felt sexual desire in that situation with that individual.
Expectations also may form as a result of other people's reactions to a
stimulus (i.e., category-based expectancies; Jones & McGillis, 1976), as
when a woman expects to feel sexual desire for her date because her
friends continually comment on his sexual attractiveness and their
own desire to engage in sexual activities with him. Still other expectations may derive from sociocultural norms about sexuality that
dictate the situations in which, and individuals for whom, it is acceptable to feel sexual desire (e.g., Gagnon & Simon, 1973; Reiss, 1986b); for
example, as we discuss below, a person may expect to experience sexual
desire for physically attractive, sexually mature individuals as opposed to unattractive, very young, or very old individuals.

⚬ Sociocultural Norms
About Sexual Desire

Sociologists have provided the most in-depth theoretical examinations of the impact of social and cultural forces on sexuality. For
example, Gagnon and Simon (e.g., 1973; Gagnon, 1974; Simon, 1974;

Simon & Gagnon, 1986) propose that a variety of sexual scripts, which evolve and are internalized and modified throughout adolescence and adulthood, define those persons and objects with whom it is acceptable to engage in sexual activity, when and where sexual activity appropriately may be conducted, and the motives or reasons an individual should possess to engage in sexual activity. Sexual scripts function as a code for directing a person's sexual actions and anticipating his or her partner's response and serve to determine the emotional reactions toward and the meanings attributed to sexual experiences. According to this perspective, sexuality is not an inherently significant aspect of human behavior. Rather, sexual phenomena become significant when they are assigned meaning by collective life (defined as sociogenic influence) or achieve meaning as the result of individual development or experience (ontogenic significance).

Reiss (e.g., 1960, 1967, 1986a, 1986b) proposed a sociological theory of sexuality that asserts that human sexuality consists of cultural scripts that are aimed at erotic arousal and that produce genital responses. Like any other social behavior, our ability to participate in sexual relationships is learned within a societal context. Because many sexual acts involve self-disclosure and yield physical pleasure, sexual interaction has an inherent social bonding power; all societies therefore have created sexual customs that place boundary mechanisms around sexuality (e.g., sexual relations within marriage). The sexual ideology characteristic of a given society shapes the interpretation placed on various aspects of sexuality, defining as "normal" or "natural" those sexual behaviors or customs that support the society's ideological views of human nature and condemning as "abnormal" or "unnatural" those activities or customs that do not conform to these beliefs. When discussing the case of premature ejaculation, for example, Reiss (1986b) writes:

> A generation ago very few people were going to therapists for treatment for premature ejaculation. The concept of premature ejaculation is based on an equalitarian view of heterosexual coital relationships. It is predominantly when the female's orgasm is of concern that a male will view himself as a premature ejaculator. He is "premature" in terms of the cultural ideal that his partner should have a coital orgasm if he does. In cultures with a more prominent double standard, such concerns are not so strongly felt. (p. 238)

Premature ejaculation and other "problems" may be largely a matter of conformity to a sexual norm that decrees that coitus should be the central sexual act for heterosexual partners and that coital orgasms, as opposed to oral or manual orgasms, are preferable. According to Reiss (1986b), the fact that this norm promotes a sexual act that produces orgasm more easily in men than in women—and that men and women prefer orgasm in coitus—demonstrates the ways in which both sexes have been indoctrinated into a "male type of sexuality" (p. 238).

Sexual desire, along with intercourse and other sexual behaviors, also exists within a social context. From the day we are born, we are bombarded by sociocultural scripts that teach us the "shoulds" and "should nots" of sexual desire. Early on, we learn who constitutes an appropriate object of our sexual desire (e.g., physically attractive, sexually mature individuals as opposed to unattractive, sexually immature individuals), the ways in which sexual desire should be communicated, the life cycle stage at which sexual desire ought to be experienced, the places and settings and even times of day when sexual desire appropriately may occur, and the amount of sexual desire we should feel for our partners and over the course of our lifetimes. Indeed, the concept of inhibited or low sexual desire is based on a cultural view of "normal" human sexuality that presupposes that both partners in a romantic relationship must experience at least some sexual desire for each other. Our ability to experience and express sexual desire probably is shaped as much by the societal recognition that we are potential sexual partners capable of experiencing sexual desire and initiating and responding to sexual overtures as it is by the other factors researchers have investigated.

❧ Specific Beliefs About Sexual Desire

In addition to learned affective expectations and sociocultural scripts about desire, the specific beliefs that men and women hold may also have important consequences for the experience and expression of sexual desire. Indeed, the sexuality literature provides at least two demonstrations that beliefs and attitudes about sexual phenomena parallel actual sexual behavior in romantic relationships. For example, research on sexual standards has identified a set of widely held beliefs about the male and female role in heterosexual sexual interaction (i.e., men initiate sexual activity, women respond to male initiation with refusal or acceptance; e.g., Reiss, 1981). These beliefs closely match the actual behavior of men and women in both dating (e.g., O'Sullivan & Byers, 1992) and marital (e.g., Byers & Heinlein, 1989) relationships. Similarly, researchers interested in sexual aggression and rape have delineated a set of stereotypic beliefs or "rape myths" (e.g., women have an unconscious wish to be raped) that not only is commonly endorsed by the American population (e.g., Burt, 1980) but that also predicts sexually aggressive behavior among young men in their ongoing dating relationships (e.g., Christopher, Owens, & Stecker, 1993; Malamuth, Sockloskie, Koss, & Tanaka, 1991). Thus, whatever their origin and whether they have basis in fact, the beliefs that men and women hold about sexual desire—its characteristic causal antecedents, manifestations, and consequences—undoubtedly have direct implications for their sexual behavior and for their relationships with actual and potential sexual partners.

Oddly enough, not a great deal is known about the beliefs that guide people's behavior with respect to sexual desire. Some researchers believe that sexual desire may mean different things to different individuals and, moreover, that sexual desire often is confused with other needs and desires. For example, both Beigel (1951) and Vandereycken (1987) suggest that a desire for sex may easily be mistaken for or mislabeled as a desire for love or intimacy. Maslow (1987) argues that sexual desire may represent a "desire to impress, or a desire for closeness, friendliness, for safety, for love, or for any combination of these" (p. 6), and Neubeck (1972) similarly noted that sexual desire may stem not only from a need for physical pleasure but also from a longing for "affection, love, intimacy, romance" (p. 52) (and from a wish to vent anger or hostility toward the partner, to relieve the boredom of everyday routine, to fulfill one's marital obligations, to assuage one's own or the partner's wounded feelings, to give pleasure to the partner, or to affirm one's own self-concept).

So what do people think about sexual desire? To answer this question, we conducted two studies (Regan & Berscheid, 1995, 1996). In the first, we examined beliefs about the nature of sexual desire—its state, its goals, and its objects; in the second, we explored beliefs about the causal antecedents of sexual desire. Below, we briefly present the results of our investigations.

Beliefs About the Nature of Sexual Desire

In response to the open-ended question, "What is sexual desire?" 142 male and female college students spontaneously generated their own definitions of sexual desire. Their definitional essays were examined for the presence of three elements: (a) whether the *state* of sexual desire was viewed as a *psychological* experience or, rather, as a *physiological* or *behavioral* experience; (b) whether a *goal* or *aim* of sexual desire was mentioned and, if so, what; and (c) whether an *object* (i.e., desired individual or other) toward whom sexual desire is directed was mentioned.

Our results indicated that, when thinking about the state of sexual desire, most participants made reference to motivational, cognitive, emotional, or similar subjective, *psychological* experiences. Specifically, 86.8% referred to motivational experiences (i.e., desire and euphemisms such as longing, urge, craving, yearning, drive, interest, need, and want); 25.7% characterized sexual desire as an emotional state (i.e., emotion, emotional attraction, or feeling); 6.6% viewed sexual desire as a cognitive state (i.e., thoughts, fantasies, wishes); and 2.9% defined the phenomenon as a specific psychological syndrome (i.e., love or passion). A mere 4.4% and 2.2% conceptualized sexual desire as a *physiological* state (i.e., arousal) or *behavioral* state (i.e., sexual activity, response), respectively. Typical responses included the following:

> Sexual desire is the *need* or the *want* to have sexual intercourse with someone. It is a *feeling* that is totally uncontrollable, a *desire*. I know that I get this feeling and I know that my friends (male) get them. I also know that my girlfriend gets them. [male, emphasis added]

> Desire is an *impulse/drive* to engage in sexual and intimate activities with another person and *wanting* to be physically and emotionally close to someone. [female, emphasis added]

> I believe sexual desire to be an inner *emotion*. It is the *wanting* or *longing* for sex or sexual relations. [female, emphasis added]

Thus, common interpretations of the term *sexual desire* among young adults appear quite consistent with the definition and discussion we presented in Chapter 2.

Interestingly, although men and women agreed about what sexual desire is, they had different perceptions of the *goal* and *object* of sexual desire. Specifically, significantly more men (70%) than women (43.1%) believed that sexual desire was aimed at sexual activity (although this was the most commonly cited goal by both sexes), and significantly more men (29.8%) than women (5.7%) specified that the desired object be physically and/or sexually attractive:

Wanting someone (opposite sex) in a physical manner. No strings attached. Just for uninhibited sexual intercourse. No relationship necessary. Just physical attraction. [male]

Sexual desire is the urge to be satisfied sexually by someone you are physically, intellectually and/or emotionally attracted to. [male]

Sexual desire is someone wanting to have sex with someone else because they find that person physically attractive, and the sex drive drives them to pursue that person. [male]

Significantly more women (34.5%) than men (13.3%) cited love or emotional intimacy as a goal of sexual desire. For example:

Sexual desire is the longing to be emotionally intimate and to express love for another person. [female]

I don't think we can limit sexual desire to only physical pleasures. Sexual desire can also include wanting to be in the company of the person of the opposite sex, desire to be able to build a relationship where the two can share feelings and thoughts, and perhaps simply wanting to be in close proximity of the person of the opposite sex. [female]

That women were more likely to associate sexual desire with the pursuit of interpersonal goals whereas men were more likely to focus on sexual goals or pleasure provides evidence for previous theoretical speculation that men and women have different orientations toward sexuality (e.g., DeLamater, 1987). These results also raised some questions. For example, if women are more likely than men to associate sexual desire with love and emotional commitment, would they also be more likely to believe that love and intimacy are important causes of female sexual desire? Moreover, if men are aware that women make this association, would they also cite those variables as determinants of sexual desire in women? What about male sexual desire? What do people believe causes men to experience feelings of desire? To address these questions, we conducted a second study.

Beliefs About the Causes of Sexual Desire

We asked a second sample of 108 men and women if they believed that there was a difference between what causes sexual desire in a man and what causes sexual desire in a woman. The majority (71.3%) claimed that there was. We then asked the participants to specify what these different causes were in a free-response format.

As illustrated in Table 5.1, our respondents generated a variety of causes, including *person* causes associated with the desiring individual (e.g., sexual fantasies, biological or hormonal processes), *partner* causes associated with the object of desire (e.g., attractive or sexy body or appearance, use of sexually explicit speech or actions), *interpersonal* causes associated with the relationship between the desiring person and the desired partner (e.g., mutual feelings of love, flirting, sexual activity), *physical environment* causes (e.g., erotic or pornographic media, romantic settings), and *social environment* causes (e.g., "socialization" practices, parental upbringing).

Participants generated relatively similar causes for male and female sexual desire. However, despite the general similarity between the sets of presumed causes, our results revealed that a significantly greater proportion of the respondents cited interpersonal or relationship causes in general for female sexual desire (53.7%) than for male sexual desire (25.7%). In addition, although the specific interpersonal cause of love was specified as a determinant of male sexual desire by fewer than 10% of the participants, love was cited by 42.1% as a cause of female sexual desire. Indeed, sexual desire in women was primarily assumed to depend on the occurrence of various interpersonal and "romantic" events in the physical environment:

TABLE 5.1 Beliefs About the Causes of Sexual Desire in Men and in Women

Causes	Male Sexual Desire (in percentages)	Female Sexual Desire (in percentages)
Person causes (e.g., sexual fantasies or thoughts, biological or hormonal processes, alcohol ingestion or drug use, sexual tension or physical need)	63.4	33.7
Partner causes (e.g., sexy or attractive body or appearance, scent or smell, personality)	53.5	34.7
Interpersonal causes (e.g., mutual feelings of love, flirting, sexual activity)	25.7	53.7
Physical environment causes (e.g., romantic settings, erotic or pornographic media, location or situation providing the opportunity for sexual activity)	23.8	35.8
Social environment causes (e.g., socialization practices, parental upbringing)	8.9	5.3

NOTE: These percentages will not sum to 100% because some participants specified more than one causal category in their free-response essays.

Thoughts of love and romance. Women tend to be more romantic. . . . Women do have sexual desires brought on by suggestive surroundings but not to the extent of men. Quiet, romantic surroundings and events seem to play a large role in sexual desire. [male]

Sexual desire in a woman, on the average, is caused by love. . . . A woman tends to be in love when she feels desire or has sexual intercourse. [male]

Being in love. Sometimes women feel sexual desire for purely physical reasons, but I think that more often it has to do with being in love. Also, I think that a lot of times women feel sexual desire through being caressed. [female]

> Often the words "I love you" will cause sexual desire in a woman. I think that if a man showers positive attention on a woman and makes her feel desirable that causes sexual desire. [female]

None of our respondents cited sexual desire as a natural or inevitable consequence of femaleness; only 33.7% believed that sexual desire arises from events that occur within women (person or intraindividual events). In contrast, when reporting their belief about the causes of male sexual desire, 63.4% generated internal, intraindividual causes. Indeed, unlike female sexual desire, sexual desire in men was assumed to require little external or interpersonal stimulation; rather, male sexual desire was depicted as an internally caused, naturally occurring, virtually inevitable consequence of being male:

> Men have what I call a "defective gene" on their DNA ladder. This "defective gene" causes sexual desire in men. I label it as defective because it sometimes interferes with a man's way of thinking and decision making. It seems that from my experience and listening to friends that guys constantly strive for their sexual desires. These same desires don't seem to be in women, thus, my conclusion that it has something to do with our DNA structure. [male]

> Hormones play a big part, I think. Watching some pornographic movie or reading anything by Anais Nin. These things cause a wish, longing, or craving to seek out sexual objects. [male]

> I'm not exactly sure what causes sexual desire in a man. I would say just about anything does. . . . In general, any man romantically involved or not tends to always have a sexual desire (or just about always). Anything seems to be able to set men off. [female]

> Simply being male is an automatic cause for sexual desire. [female]

As the above examples illustrate, the men and women in our study had similar perceptions about what causes sexual desire in their own and the other sex—both believed that female sexual desire was caused primarily by interpersonal factors and that male sexual desire was generally caused by innate, internal factors. However, although no sex differences in *beliefs* were revealed, we did find a somewhat surprising sex difference with regard to possible *knowledge* about the causes of sexual desire. Specifically, whereas only one woman had difficulty generating a response to the open-ended questions about the causes of male and female sexual desire, 11.5% of the men were unable to generate at least one cause of male sexual desire and 23.1% could not provide even one cause of female sexual desire. That this state of affairs was somewhat frustrating to our male respondents can be seen in the following responses:

> You know, to answer this would be out of touch with my knowledge. I know this is vague, but, well, so is my idea of the cause of sexual desire in women. The environment must have a role somewhere.

> I find this question a bit humorous because I don't believe that men will ever know the answer.

> If I knew the answer to that I would have an extremely happy relationship.

> Obviously I don't know the answer or there would be more women desiring me.

> I don't know. Truly if I did then I would be the town gigolo.

This finding tentatively suggests that women may have a more complete understanding of the dynamics of sexual desire than men—or at least they *think* they do.

How men and women experience and express sexual desire is undoubtedly influenced by their beliefs and assumptions about what sexual desire is and what events trigger its occurrence, as well as by affective expectations and sociocultural norms about desire. Other internal, psychological factors, discussed below, also may be associated with sexual desire.

ஊ Personality Variables

The idea that sexuality and personality are intertwined is a venerable one. Freud (e.g., 1908/1963a) viewed sexual drive or instinct as the motivating force behind personality development, and Krafft-

Ebing (1886/1945) believed that aberrant sexual behavior was a function of deep psychopathology. Today, research suggests that some psychological variables may moderate the amount of sexual desire an individual experiences. For example, erotophobia-erotophilia, defined as "the disposition to respond to sexual cues along a negative-positive dimension of affect and evaluation" (Fisher et al., 1988, p. 124), may be associated with sexual desire. This personality disposition is presumably learned during childhood and adolescence through socialization experiences in which sexuality is paired with punishments or rewards. Fisher and Gray (1988) administered the Sexual Opinion Survey, a 21-item personality scale that assesses erotophobia-erotophilia, and a questionnaire about sexual experiences to 50 couples during late pregnancy. Each couple's sexual experiences were reassessed 2 months after delivery. Erotophilic women reported more sexual interest than did their erotophobic counterparts, both while pregnant and in the postpartum period. Specifically, correlational analyses revealed that women's (but not men's) erotophobia-erotophilia scores were significantly correlated with their self-reported "interest in sexual activity" at both assessment times.

Other researchers, in an attempt to explore and clarify the relationship between personality and sexual desire, have examined the psychological characteristics of individuals with sexual desire disorders. This research generally finds little to no relationship between desire and global (maladaptive) personality constructs. For example, Schreiner-Engel and Schiavi (1986) compared the lifetime psychopathology and current psychological profiles of 46 physically healthy men and women with a presenting complaint of inhibited sexual desire (ISD) with those of 36 matched controls. Not only did none of the ISD group meet criteria for a current diagnosis of any anxiety or psychotic disorder, but an examination of participants' responses to a self-report inventory revealed that the ISD and control groups did not differ on a global index of current psychological distress. In addition, no differences were found between men and women with ISD and their controls in lifetime diagnoses of various personality and anxiety disorders, including schizophrenia, manic disorder, panic disorder, generalized anxiety, Briquet's disorder, antisocial personality, obsessive-compulsive disorder, and phobic disorder. Similarly, Stuart, Hammond, and Pett (1986) found that 51 women with ISD provided Minnesota Multiphasic Personality Inventory (MMPI) profiles within normal limits, and their scores did not differ from those of a group of 27 non-ISD women on any of the MMPI's 10 clinical scales (e.g., Hypochondriasis, Paranoia, Schizophrenia, Hypomania). These results were corroborated by Safir and Almagor (1991), who reported that the MMPI profiles of 10 women diagnosed with hypoactive sexual desire disorder or sexual aversion disorder were within normal ranges on all of the clinical scales but the Schizophrenia scale.

In general, then, some individual difference variables may moderate the experience of sexual desire; however, the absence (and, by extension, the presence) of sexual desire does not appear to be strongly associated with maladaptive personality variables.

▶ Personal Experiences: Sexual Trauma

In addition to personality characteristics, an individual's previous sexual experiences may be associated with the experience of sexual desire. For example, a growing body of clinical and empirical literature links sexual abuse with decreased sexual desire. Craine, Henson, Colliver, and MacLean (1988) interviewed 105 women in a state mental hospital who ranged in age from 13 to 81. Their results revealed that significantly more women with a history of sexual abuse in childhood or adolescence (48% of 54) indicated experiencing a "loss of interest in or enjoyment of sex" than did women who had not been abused (22% of 51). Similarly, Briere (1984) noted a decreased "sex drive" in 42% of his sample of women who had been sexually abused as children, compared with 29% of a control group of nonvictims. A comprehensive review by Browne and Finkelhor (1986) of research conducted on the impact of early sexual abuse indicates that depression is one of the most common symptoms reported by adults molested as children; as we will discuss next, depression and other negative emotional reactions may partly account for the decreased sexual desire seen in individuals who have been sexually abused.

✿ Mood

Retrospective questionnaire and prospective studies of depressed individuals and people with sexual desire disorders, clinical interviews, and menstrual cycle studies of women who experience cyclical mood changes suggest that mood and desire are intricately connected. Although an association has been noted between some types of mania and increased sexual desire (e.g., Kaplan, 1979; Young, Schreiber, & Nysewander, 1983), most research in this area has focused on depression. Whether feeling temporarily "down" or suffering from clinical depression, both men and women are less likely to feel and to express sexual desire, to interpret their experiences in a pleasant sexual manner, and to initiate sexual behavior than when they are under the influence of a positive mood, are generally feeling well, and have access to high levels of energy. For example, Howell et al.'s (1987) analysis of retrospective questionnaire and daily log data revealed that depressed men reported a significantly lower level of sexual interest than normal controls and experienced sexual interest on significantly fewer days; similarly, the depressive symptoms reported by the 274 menopausal women in Channon and Ballinger's (1986) study were significantly associated with low scores on a "libido" index that included ratings of sexual desire (also see Mathew & Weinman, 1982; Thase et al., 1988). In addition, clinical surveys consistently report reduced sexual interest in 50% to 90% of depressed individuals (e.g., Beck, 1967; Casper et al., 1985; Hamilton, 1980; Woodruff, Murphy, & Herjanic, 1967).

A second major source of evidence for the relationship between mood and sexual desire is provided by menstrual cycle studies of women who experience cyclical mood changes. Bancroft, Sanders, and their colleagues (e.g., Bancroft et al., 1983; Sanders, Warner, Backstrom, & Bancroft, 1983; Warner & Bancroft, 1988) have found evidence that women with marked cyclical mood change experience a strong associated cyclical pattern of sexual feelings such that negative "well-being" or mood tends to be associated with low levels of sexual desire, whereas positive well-being and high levels of sexual desire are more likely to co-occur. For example, Sanders et al. (1983) analyzed daily diaries of mood, physical state, and sexual interest (specifically, how sexual each woman felt in terms of interest in or desire for sexual expression or activity and how pleasant she found thoughts about any form of sexual activity to be at that moment) kept by women who had sought treatment for severe premenstrual syndrome (PMS), women with a history of PMS who had not sought treatment, and women without PMS. Analyses revealed that those women who experienced marked increases and decreases in depression and mood dimensions such as fatigue and aggression at various points throughout the menstrual cycle experienced associated decreases and increases, respectively, in sexual interest (i.e., interest in and desire for sexual expression or activity, pleasantness ratings of thoughts of sexual activity).

Additional evidence for the proposed relationship between mood and sexuality comes from studies of individuals suffering from loss or lack of desire. Schreiner-Engel and Schiavi (1986) compared 46 married subjects (22 men and 24 women) with a primary DSM-III diagnosis of global ISD with 36 matched controls on questionnaire and interview measures of lifetime and current psychopathology. Although none of the ISD or control subjects met criteria for a current diagnosis of any affective disorder, significantly more ISD men (73%) than control men (32%) and significantly more ISD women (71%) than control women (27%) met the criteria for lifetime histories of affective disorders. In terms of mood disorders alone, 55% of the ISD men and 50% of the ISD women compared with 32% of the control men and 27% of the control women, respectively, had had episodes of major depression and/or intermittent depression in the past. In addition, 88% of the ISD men with lifetime diagnoses of affective disorder retrospectively reported that their loss of sexual desire developed concurrently with or subsequent to their initial depressive episode, and 100% of the women in the ISD condition reported having lost interest in sexual activity during or following their first episode of affective illness.

❧ Emotional State

In addition to documentation about the association between depression and desire, the clinical literature also contains numerous case studies that illustrate the negative impact of emotional experiences such as anger or hostility, anxiety, and stress on sexual desire. For example, based on her examination of men and women with sexual desire disorders, Kaplan (1979) hypothesized that inhibited sexual desire may result from anger and anxiety. Sources of anxiety include fears of rejection and intimacy, as well as performance fears; anger frequently stems from envy of the sexual partner as well as poor communication and power conflicts. According to Kaplan, the experience of anger and anxiety rapidly—and usually automatically—activates an emotional "turn off" mechanism that suppresses sexual desire. Trudel (1991) and Arnett et al. (1986) similarly suggest that negative affects such as anxiety or anger stemming from occupational, interpersonal, or intrapersonal conflict may elicit a stress response that causes diminished sexual desire.

However, other researchers believe that some individuals may respond to anxiety, anger, and other "negative" emotional states with *increased* sexual desire. Hatfield and Rapson (1987) hypothesize that the effect of anxiety on sexual desire may depend on the particular situation one is in and the specific partner with whom one is interacting. For example, these researchers suggest that anxiety about performing with a rude or insensitive sexual partner may destroy sexual desire, whereas anxiety stemming from the uncertainty that an attractive partner will respond to one's sexual advances may contribute to sexual desire.

Indeed, some social psychological theory and research suggest that arousal stemming from anxiety-, anger-, or other emotion-provoking events can, under appropriate circumstances, increase sexual desire. Schachter (1964) theorized that all emotions have a common set of underlying physiological events and that individuals differentiate between the various emotions by attending to the context in which they experience physiological arousal and then labeling their experience accordingly. One implication of this theory is that sexual attraction can be increased by any extraneous source of physiological arousal that coincides with exposure to a potential sexual partner (for an extension of Schachter's theory of emotion to the development of romantic love or attraction, see Berscheid & Walster, 1974a). Dutton and Aron (1974) were the first to conduct an experiment specifically designed to test this hypothesis. These researchers exposed undergraduate men to an arousing, fear-eliciting stimulus in the form of a shaky suspension bridge or to a nonarousing solid bridge. The aroused men produced stories in response to a Thematic Appercep-tion Test card that contained significantly greater amounts of sexual imagery than the unaroused men. Similarly, a second study (repli-cated by Allen, Kenrick, Linder, & McCall, 1989) revealed that men who were expecting to receive a painful electric shock reported a greater desire to ask a female confederate out on a date and to kiss her than did nonanxious men who anticipated only a mild shock. White, Fishbein, and Rutstein (1981) demonstrated that the valence of the arousal may be unimportant. In their experiments, men were aroused neutrally through exercise, positively through exposure to an audio-taped comedy sketch, or negatively though exposure to an audio-taped mutilation scene. After being aroused, participants watched a videotape of an attractive female confederate they expected to meet after viewing the tape. Compared with nonaroused controls, all of the aroused men scored higher on a four-item attraction index (i.e., con-federate's physical attractiveness and sexiness, participant's desire to date and to kiss her).

The aforementioned research certainly suggests that extraneous arousal may enhance sexual desire for another person. However, Bozman and Beck (1991) have conducted the only experiment to date that specifically examines the effects of anger and anxiety on sexual desire. In their experiment, 24 psychologically and physically healthy undergraduate men listened to three audiotapes that contained iden-tical descriptions of three levels of sexual intimacy (i.e., caressing, foreplay, intercourse) between a man and woman. The audiotapes differed with respect to verbal statements made by the woman and self-statements or thoughts made by the man during each level of sexual activity, and each was designed to evoke a different emotional state in the participants. Anxiety in the participants was elicited by hearing performance demands stated by the woman and self-state-ments made by the man in which he questioned his sexual ability. Anger was elicited by an audiotape in which the woman made state-ments of annoyance and the man made statements reflecting his irritation with her. The third audiotape was a control condition and contained statements and self-statements appropriate during a sexual encounter between two people. Sexual desire was assessed via a subjective rating dial that consisted of a potentiometer driven by a mechanical dial. Participants were instructed to rate the intensity of their sexual desire, and not their physical arousal or penile tumescence, continuously throughout the session using the dial and a scale ranging from 0 (no sexual desire at all) to 100 (intense sexual desire). In addition, participants indicated their emotional state (e.g., tension-anxiety, depression, anger-hostility, confusion-bewilderment) on 5-point rating scales immediately following the presentation of each audiotape; analysis of these data indicated that the experimental manipulation was effective. For example, men reported experiencing a significantly greater amount of anger-hostility after listening to the audiotape designed to elicit anger than after listening to the other two audiotapes. Experimental data were analyzed in three time blocks of 150 seconds, each based on changes in the level of sexual intimacy in the audiotaped interactions. Although sexual desire increased over time (that is, as the stimuli progressed), results indicated significant differences in sexual desire between conditions. Specifically, participants experienced significantly less sexual desire while listening to the anger audiotape than they did while listening to the anxiety or control audiotapes, and they reported significantly less sexual desire during the anxiety audiotape than they did during the control audiotape. These results indicate that negative emotional states do impair or diminish the experience of sexual desire, and they also suggest that some negative emotions (i.e., anger) may be more destructive than others (i.e., anxiety) with respect to this particular aspect of sexuality.

In sum, the existing literature indicates that arousal that is non-sexual in nature may increase sexual desire. However, if the source of arousal is negative and is sexual in nature (i.e., stems from anxiety about one's own sexual ability or attractiveness or fears about the partner's response to one's sexual advances), decreased sexual desire may result.

❧ Conclusions

In this chapter, we considered the mental or psychological causes of sexual desire. Many of these factors, although arising from within or controlled by the desiring individual, have interpersonal implications and are intricately connected to relationship events. For example, the sociocultural assumption that sexual desire appropriately is experienced for a (sexually mature) romantic partner, the belief that one of the goals of sexual desire is emotional intimacy, and the affective expectation that one usually feels desire in this particular situation and for this particular partner may cause a person to interpret his or her feelings of desire as "love" and the partner's wish to engage in sexual activity as a sign of romantic interest and emotional commitment. Similarly, many emotions are experienced within the context of a specific relationship—we reviewed research that suggests that anger and hostility felt toward the partner may reduce sexual interest in that person. Thus, it seems natural that we should continue our discussion of the causes of desire by next considering the interpersonal and external factors associated with the experience of sexual desire.

6

Sexual Desire
The Partner and
the Relationship

In the quest to identify the causal antecedents of sexual desire, researchers have given most of their attention to internal or intraindividual factors. In the last three chapters, we reviewed research on the physical (e.g., hormonal processes, age, health, drug use) and mental (e.g., beliefs, expectations, emotions, personality) variables that may affect an individual and his or her feelings of sexual desire. However, sexual desire also is affected by external events and phenomena. In the present chapter, we explore these external causes of desire, including characteristics associated with the partner or desired other, factors located in the physical surroundings or environment, and factors that reside in the relationship between the desiring individual and the desired other.

Sexually Desirable Partner Characteristics

The majority of research on partner preferences has focused on delineating the characteristics that men and women seek and prefer in potential *romantic* partners—that is, partners with whom one would form a long-term, emotionally intimate, committed relationship (for reviews of this large literature, see Buss, 1995; Kenrick, 1994; Surra, 1990). In fact, only recently have researchers and theorists recognized that the characteristics that determine a person's desirability as a long-term romantic partner may differ in quality and quantity from those that determine his or her *sexual* desirability.

Theoretical Perspectives on Sexual Desirability

A consideration of several theoretical perspectives suggests that certain characteristics might be viewed as particularly important components of sexual desirability.

Social Context Perspectives. Social context frameworks focus on proximal causal mechanisms—causes located in the contemporary social, cultural, and historical milieu—that may influence our partner preferences. In particular, social psychologists and sociologists have explored the ways in which social and cultural scripts (e.g., Gagnon & Simon, 1973; Reiss, 1986b; see Chapter 5) as well as the patterns of reinforcement and punishment that men and women receive for their sexual behavior (e.g., Mischel, 1966) shape our beliefs and expectations about sexuality. Applied to sexual desire, these perspectives suggest that sexual desire appropriately is experienced for and directed toward individuals who are reproductively mature, physically attractive, and sexually receptive: In Western cultures, it is not considered acceptable to desire sexual activity with preadolescent, unattractive, unwilling partners, and men and women who do evince these desires are indirectly or directly discouraged from voicing and behaving in service of them.

In addition, social context theories suggest that some characteristics may be differentially important in determining male and female sexual desirability. For example, social role theory (e.g., Eagly, 1987; Eagly & Karau, 1991) posits that people develop expectations for their own and others' behavior based on their beliefs about sex-appropriate behavior and attributes. Such beliefs and expectations are assumed to arise from the distribution of men and women into different social roles in natural settings; specifically, the sexes are believed to possess attributes suited for the roles each typically occupies (although this is changing, the male role is primarily occupational and economic, whereas the female role is traditionally domestic). To the extent that people prefer others to behave in accordance with existing sex role stereotypes, traditionally "male" characteristics and attributes (e.g., career orientation, high-paying job) may be viewed as particularly important determinants of male sexual desirability, and traditionally "female" characteristics and attributes (e.g., display an attractive appearance) may be considered significant features of female sexual desirability.

Evolutionary Perspectives. Evolutionary frameworks focus on distal causal mechanisms that might influence partner preferences—evolved psychological heuristics that were selected because they overcame obstacles to reproduction located in the human ancestral past and therefore maximized genetic fitness. Originating from Charles Darwin's (1859, 1871) work, these perspectives assume that the "goal" of human mating relationships is reproduction—the act of (heterosexual) sexual intercourse and the production of viable offspring (that is, offspring who survive to reach reproductive maturity). Due to the relatively slow reproductive cycle of our species (e.g., the long gestational period, the significant amount of parental care required by offspring), men and women must exercise some care when selecting a potential reproductive partner. Several factors are posited to influence partner choice, including the potential partner's physical or genetic fitness; his or her emotional fitness or willingness to invest in the reproductive partner, the reproductive relationship, and resulting offspring; and paternity certainty or the estimated likelihood that offspring produced with a particular partner are indeed one's own (e.g., Buss & Schmitt, 1993; Cunningham, Druen, & Barbee, 1997; Gangestad & Simpson, 1990; Kenrick, Sadalla, Groth, & Trost, 1990; Trivers, 1972).

Mating relationships can range from the extremely casual and short term to the highly committed and long term (e.g., Buss & Schmitt, 1993; Kenrick et al., 1990), and some of these factors may become particularly important in certain types of relationships. For example, when considering a potential long-term partner, emotional fitness may be of paramount importance (e.g., Cunningham et al., 1997); when evaluating a potential short-term sexual partner, physical and genetic fitness may be of primary importance (e.g., Gangestad, 1993). In the latter mating context, both men and women might be expected to prefer a sexually mature, healthy individual who is capable of reproduction and will pass on "good" genetic material to any resulting offspring. Insofar as physical appearance is presumed to indicate underlying genetic fitness and health (e.g., Buss & Kenrick, 1998; Fisher, 1958; Gangestad, 1993), appearance may be a particularly important determinant of male and female sexual desirability.

In addition, some features may be differentially important in determining the sexual desirability of each sex. For example, Trivers's (1972) parental investment model posits that women, who invest more direct physiological resources in their offspring than men (e.g., contributing body nutrients during pregnancy and lactation), will be more sensitive to resource limitations and thus particularly attentive to a reproductive partner's social status, which is presumably related to his ability to provide resources in the form of food, material possessions, and physical protection. Building on this model, subsequent evolutionary theorists have suggested that women will prefer as short-term sex partners those men who can and who will provide immediate resources (e.g., Buss & Schmitt, 1993; Kenrick et al., 1990; Wright, 1994). Thus, social position, material possessions, and demonstrated or potential resource-accruing ability may be a significant component of male sexual desirability.

In sum, both social context and evolutionary frameworks suggest that certain characteristics are important features of sexual desirability. We turn now from the theoretical to the empirical. What constellation of features do men and women actually use to evaluate another individual's sexual desirability?

What Characteristics Determine Sexual Desirability?

In Chapter 5, we described some of our research on men's and women's beliefs about sexual desire. In addition to examining assumptions about the causes of sexual desire, we also asked our participants to describe the specific characteristics in men and women that cause sexual desire in the opposite sex (Regan & Berscheid, 1995, Study 2). Typical answers to the question "What characteristics in a woman cause a man to experience sexual desire for her?" included the following:

> I think men want women to be willing, attractive, and interesting. It makes the desire stronger when he knows she wants the same thing, although not being able to get sex from her sometimes will do the same thing. Physically, I think a desirable woman would be soft, yet athletic, not fat, but not overly thin, with lots of curves and a nice face. A woman who is experienced and enjoys sex is more desirable than either an inexperienced, shy woman or else an overly experienced, "easy" woman. [male]

> Her appearance. Nothing else is needed. A man can be with any woman as long as he thinks she looks good. The easiest way to get a man interested in a woman is for his friends to say how good the girl looks. I truly feel that besides the body—no other characteristics are needed. [male]

> Definitely an attitude that portrays that she wants "it." Flirtation seems to help men become more interested. A confident characteristic that would suggest that she is good at "it." Overall attractiveness (skinny, tall, nice smile). [female]

> Could be very thin with long, thin legs, long hair, white teeth. Could be voluptuous—I guess what I'm getting down to is physical attraction (very seldom is it intellectual!). Also . . . Easy helps! For some men, if a woman appears to be sexually adventurous, even if she isn't particularly attractive, he'll give it a shot. Also, many men go for women who *aren't* easy. Challenge, the seduction (and once he gets her, the desire is over!). [female]

The question "What characteristics in a man cause a woman to experience sexual desire for him?" elicited similar responses from our participants:

> I think a well-built, strong man would cause desire as opposed to a sloppy, overweight guy or a really skinny guy. I think women desire a guy who is open, honest, and is interested in pleasing them, instead of the opposite. I also think a woman desires men who appreciate

her sexual appetites/preferences over ones who force their own wishes on her. Physical qualities would probably include muscles, and cleanliness or being well-groomed. [male]

Women like men to be funny and caring. A major thing for women is that they want a man to be sensitive to their needs as women. Physical attractiveness is important to women, although they don't tend to show this as much as men do. I wish I knew more about this question myself—believe me! [male]

A great fit body, and nice clothes. This doesn't mean that's all I'm looking for, but to be sexually attracted—yes. [female]

Based on physical characteristics I would say the way a person looks such as his face, eyes, lips, and a well-toned body. A man must be caring, kind, and gentle. He must be able to show his feelings and let you know he cares about you. [female]

This research was designed to identify the constellation of partner characteristics believed to produce sexual desire. It is apparent from our participants' responses that a number of different attributes are considered sexually desirable. It is equally apparent that some of these characteristics are perceived to be more strongly associated with sexual desirability than others. Below, we review research that has examined the association between specific partner characteristics and sexual attractiveness.

Physical Attractiveness

According to the men and women who participated in our previously described study, a physically attractive appearance is the single most important desire-causing quality a person can possess. The notion that appearance is associated with sexual attractiveness is not new. For example, in speculating about the human ancestral condition, the evolutionary theorist Charles Darwin (1871) suggested that "both sexes, if the females as well as the males were permitted to exert any choice, would have chosen their partners, not for mental charms, or property, or social position, but almost solely from external appearance" (p. 368). Echoes of this belief can be found in later work by Albert Ellis, one of the first psychologists to systematically examine how and why a person's (in particular, a woman's) physical appearance determines his or her value as a social, romantic, and sexual object. Ellis (1954) devoted much of his work, aptly titled *The American Sexual Tragedy*, to exploring the "great American prerequisite to sex, love, and marriage" (p. 16)—namely, feminine pulchritude—and the myth, relentlessly promulgated by the popular press, that there exists a universal ideal of physical beauty to which all women (and, to some extent, men) should and must measure up if they wish to attract a sexual, romantic, or marriage partner.

Indeed, social psychological researchers interested in physical appearance have found overwhelming evidence for the existence of a pervasive physical attractiveness stereotype, perhaps best illustrated by the slightly cynical and oft-quoted phrase, "What is beautiful is good" (Dion, Berscheid, & Walster, 1972). Physically attractive men and women, for example, are believed to possess more socially desirable personality characteristics and are viewed as more likable, well-adjusted, and socially skilled than their less attractive counterparts (e.g., Berscheid & Walster, 1974b; Dion et al., 1972; Goldman & Lewis, 1977). Beauty also is associated with social status (e.g., Kalick, 1988), and beautiful others are preferred as dating or romantic partners (e.g., Walster, Aronson, Abrahams, & Rottman, 1966) and are presumed to marry earlier, achieve happier marriages, and make more competent spouses (e.g., Dion et al., 1972). Occupationally, attractive persons are expected to perform better and are ascribed higher employment potential and more prestigious jobs (e.g., Cash, Gillen, & Burns, 1977; Gilmore, Beehr, & Love, 1986).

In addition, what is beautiful also appears to be what is sexually desirable. For example, men and women in a study conducted by Suman (1990) perceived physically attractive opposite-sex strangers as more sexually attractive than less physically attractive others. In addition, Feingold's (1992) meta-analysis of the extensive experimental and correlational research on attractiveness revealed that physically attractive men and women are perceived as sexually warmer and more responsive, and also report having engaged in a greater variety of sexual activities (and, for women, at earlier ages), than less attractive individuals. To the extent that beautiful others are assumed to be sexually welcoming, it is not surprising that they also are preferred as sexual partners. Indeed, we (Regan & Berscheid, 1997) asked a sample of men and women to rank order a set of 22 characteristics in terms of desirability in a potential sexual partner, defined as "someone with whom you might want to engage in sexual activity (e.g., kissing, "making out," intercourse)." An attractive physical appearance was the characteristic most preferred by men and women when considering a sex partner. Similar results have been reported by Kenrick, Groth, Trost, and Sadalla (1993), Nevid (1984), and Regan (1998a, 1998c; also see Regan, Levin, Sprecher, Cate, & Christopher, 1998). In addition, the physical attractiveness of an opposite-sex stimulus person predicted men's and women's expressed willingness to "have sex with" that person in a study conducted by Townsend and Levy (1990).

In short, research in a number of areas provides strong evidence that a person's physical attractiveness is an important factor in arousing both male and female sexual desire.

Physique

Much of the physical attractiveness literature has focused on facial features to the relative exclusion of other morphological variables (see Berscheid, 1985, for additional discussion). However, body characteristics also may be important to individuals when assessing their own or another's sexual attractiveness. For example, Franzoi and Herzog (1987) asked men and women to evaluate the importance of various body parts in determining the attractiveness of same- and other-sex persons. There was substantial agreement among respondents; specifically, both men and women judged physical features associated with upper body strength (e.g., muscular strength, waist, arms, chest, width of shoulders, body build) as important determinants of male attractiveness, and both sexes viewed characteristics associated with weight (e.g., waist, thighs, buttocks, body build, weight, appearance of stomach) as important aspects of female attractiveness.

Research substantiates the contention that the structure and form of the body are potent determinants of attraction. In their review of the interpersonal attraction literature, for example, Berscheid and Walster (1974b) posit as a cardinal principle of heterosexual date selection that the man must be as tall as or taller than the woman, and research has demonstrated that women indeed express a preference for taller men and men a preference for shorter women as dates (e.g., Shepperd & Strathman, 1989). Other research suggests that, for men, being short is more of a liability than being tall is an asset. Graziano, Brothen, and Berscheid (1978) provided women with information about the height of men portrayed in photographs. Trend analyses revealed that women preferred the tall male over the short male; however, the medium-height males were rated as more attractive and as more desirable as dates than both short and tall males. Similarly, Jackson and Ervin (1992) reported that men and women rated short persons of *both* sexes as less physically attractive than average height or tall individuals.

As well as height, body shape may be related to a person's perceived attractiveness. For example, men prefer and view as more attractive the "hourglass" appearance of normal-weight female figures with a low waist-to-hip ratio (an index of body fat distribution quantified by computing a ratio of the circumference of the waist to the circumference of the hips; e.g., Singh, 1993; Singh & Luis, 1995; also see Gitter, Lomranz, Saxe, & Bar-Tal, 1983). Women prefer a tapering "V" physique in men (e.g., Lavrakas, 1975) and assign higher attractiveness ratings to normal-weight men with a typically masculine (as opposed to feminine) waist-to-hip ratio (e.g., Singh, 1995).

General body size appears to be a particularly important determinant of physical and sexual attractiveness. Both men and women perceive thinner or normal weight people of both sexes to be more physically attractive than extremely thin or very overweight individuals (e.g., Clayson & Klassen, 1989; Davis-Pyles, Conger, & Conger, 1990; Furnham & Radley, 1989; Lamb, Jackson, Cassiday, & Priest, 1993; Singh, 1993; Wiggins, Wiggins, & Conger, 1968). In addition, a recent study conducted by Regan (1996b) suggests that obese individuals are not perceived to be as sexually attractive as normal weight individuals or believed to be as capable of experiencing sexual desire, attracting a sexual partner, and developing a satisfying sexual relationship. In this study, men and women received information about another man ("Jim") or woman ("Julie") who was characterized either as obese or normal weight. They then made several inferences about the target individual's sexual characteristics and interpersonal sexual experiences. Participants believed that a normal weight woman and a normal weight man would have highly similar sexual characteristics and interpersonal, sexual experiences. However, they viewed the obese Jim as less likely to have a current sex partner and as less sexually attractive and desirable as a sex partner than the normal weight Jim. Similarly, participants perceived the obese Julie as less sexually attractive, desirable, skilled, warm, and responsive than the normal weight Julie, and they also viewed her as less likely to experience both subjective, psychological sexual events (i.e., sexual desire) and overt, sexual behaviors (e.g., intercourse, kissing). This pattern of results strongly suggests that body size not only is perceived as an important aspect of sexual attractiveness for both men and women but also is viewed as an important predictor of interpersonal sexual experiences.

In short, moderation appears to be what is beautiful and potentially sexually desirable: With few exceptions, the extremes in stature, body shape, and body size are disliked. Indeed, an early study on men's preferences with regard to the size of female breasts, buttocks, and legs revealed that an arbitrarily determined "standard" figure with average-sized breasts, buttocks, and legs was evaluated more positively than a figure whose features were much larger or much smaller (Wiggins et al., 1968); another study indicated that women prefer men with an average or "typical" body build (i.e., medium frame with balanced bone, muscle, and fat) over those with balanced but smaller frames and those with bulkier, thickly muscled physiques (Salusso-Deonier, Markee, & Pedersen, 1993; also see Beck, Ward-Hull, & McLear, 1976).

Physique Display

Research conducted in the realm of physical appearance generally relies on a trait perspective that defines appearance as a unitary construct composed of and limited to one's unadorned, genetically determined features (in particular, one's facial features). This approach ignores the possibility that an individual's features can be and frequently are changed in accordance with personal taste or social convention. Some researchers, therefore, have proposed the adoption of a self-presentational conceptualization of appearance, one that includes not only physical features but the medium through which these features are presented (e.g., Cash, Rissi, & Chapman, 1985;

Schlenker, 1980). According to this perspective, illustrated by Schlenker (1980), an individual's physical or personal appearance is composed of physical features, makeup (cosmetic items directly applied to the face or body), and wardrobe (clothes, jewelry, and other adornments that are physically secured to the person).

Because appearance is at least partially self-constructed, it becomes possible to create a more or less sexually desirable image, thereby influencing the perceptions and behavior of others. Indeed, at least one study suggests that the way in which an individual presents or displays his or her physical attributes may affect his or her perceived sexual attractiveness. Hill, Nocks, and Gardner (1987) asked college students to view photographs of opposite-sex stimulus persons who wore clothing that either accentuated or de-emphasized their physique (e.g., ties and buttoned shirts versus unbuttoned shirts or revealing tank tops for men; buttoned shirts, loose sweaters, or jackets versus tank tops, tube tops, or low-cut, clingy dresses for women). The results revealed that men found a physique-revealing woman to be significantly more attractive as a sexual partner than a physique-concealing woman, whereas women perceived a physique-concealing man to be more attractive as a sexual partner than a man whose clothing revealed his physique.

Social Status and Dominance

Recall that social context and evolutionary theorists suggest that characteristics related to social status or resource acquisition may also affect a person's—specifically, a man's—sexual desirability. Certainly the *male* participants in our study on desire-causing characteristics believed this assumption to be accurate:

> Women are more attracted or feel more sexual desire for men in high status positions. For example I believe money and assets are more important in the facilitation of sexual desire in women than men. If a man has a nice car, good home, lots of money, belongs to a fraternity, or is a CEO, then he has a great chance to evoke sexual desire in his female counterpart. [male]

> His personal appearance. Also, if money making skills are a characteristic, then that causes sexual desire. [male]

However, our female participants did not agree—in fact, less than 4% (as opposed to 27% of the men) cited a man's social status and financial or material resources as important causes of sexual desire in women. Subsequent research (Regan, 1998a, 1998c; Regan & Berscheid, 1997; Regan, Levin, et al., 1998) provides corroborating evidence that attributes related to social position (e.g., social status, popularity, material possessions, wealth, good earning capacity) are not considered particularly important to women (or to men) when considering a partner for a short-term, sexual relationship (although women tend to emphasize these attributes more than men when considering a long-term, romantic relationship).

However, other research suggests the opposite. For example, men and women in Townsend and Levy's (1990) study read a profile of an opposite-sex individual who was variously described as a doctor (high social status), high school teacher (medium social status), or waiter/waitress (low social status). The target person's level of ascribed social status predicted women's, but not men's, stated willingness to engage in sexual activity with him or her. Similar results were reported by Sadalla, Kenrick, and Vershure (1987), who investigated whether dominance (defined as an individual's relative position in a social hierarchy) would increase perceived sexual attractiveness. In that study, women college students rated men who engaged in high-dominance behaviors during a videotaped interaction (e.g., sat in a relaxed posture, employed higher rates of gesturing and lower rates of head nodding) and men who were described as dominant in a written scenario as more sexually attractive than nondominant men. Dominance did not affect men's perceptions of women's sexual attractiveness.

Recent research by Graziano, Jensen-Campbell, and their research team (e.g., Graziano, Jensen-Campbell, Todd, & Finch, 1997; Jensen-Campbell, Graziano, & West, 1995) may shed some light on the seemingly contradictory evidence about the relationship between dominance and sexual attractiveness. Specifically, these authors suggest that women may view male dominance as an expression of agentic behavior; that is, as reflecting an ability to actively make choices and deal effectively with others. Without additional, qualifying information (as in the Sadalla et al., 1987, study), women generally may view a man who demonstrates dominant/agentic behavior as desirable. However, male dominance behavior may become less attractive to women if it occurs in the presence of other personality traits or behavioral tendencies (e.g., competitiveness, selfishness). To test this hypothesis, Jensen-Campbell and her colleagues (1995, Study 2) constructed video scripts to manipulate dominance and agreeableness. In their study, women participants watched one of four videotaped interactions involving a man who displayed either high or low levels of dominant behavior (as in the Sadalla et al., 1987, study) and high or low levels of agreeable behavior toward a confederate. Their results indicated that men who were not agreeable (i.e., who criticized the opinions of their interaction partner, were insensitive to his or her perspective, and were not especially interpersonally warm) were not considered sexually attractive, irrespective of their levels of dominant behavior. However, dominance significantly increased the perceived sexual attractiveness of men who were *high* in agreeableness; a highly dominant man who behaved in a personable, interpersonally warm manner was considered more sexually attractive than a nondominant man who demonstrated the same highly agreeable behavior. Thus, a highly dominant man who was not agreeable was not considered especially sexually attractive, whereas a highly dominant man who also was agreeable was viewed as quite sexually desirable (in fact, women gave the highest sexual attractiveness ratings to the high-dominant/high-agreeable man).

Similar results have been reported by Cunningham and his colleagues (e.g., Cunningham, Barbee, Graves, Lundy, & Lister, 1996). These researchers asked women to evaluate, among other things, the likelihood that they would have sexual intercourse with a male target while on a date. The male targets were described as possessing either prosocial or nonprosocial personality characteristics (e.g., the prosocial target ostensibly achieved scores on a moral development task that indicated honesty and integrity as opposed to dishonesty) and as having high or low resources (e.g., the high-resource target expected a modest earned annual income supplemented by a $200,000/year trust fund due to his parents' lottery winnings). These two attributes interacted to influence the male target's sexual desirability. Specifically, women indicated that they would be more likely to have sex while on a date with the prosocial and wealthy man than they would while on a date with the prosocial, *non*wealthy man. However, they were unwilling to consider sex on a date with a man who possessed nonprosocial personality characteristics, regardless of his level of wealth. As before, then, resources alone did not increase a man's sexual attractiveness; only when coupled with other, positive attributes did wealth influence sexual desirability.

What can we conclude? Well, in general, research suggests that social status, resources, dominance, and related characteristics are not strongly related to a *woman's* sexual attractiveness. In addition, by themselves, these attributes do not appear strongly associated with a *man's* sexual desirability. However, when linked with other, positive traits or characteristics (including prosociality and agreeableness), status, wealth, and position may become relatively important determinants of male sexual attractiveness.

Interpersonal Behavior

As indicated from our previous discussion, behaviors that demonstrate interpersonal responsiveness and warmth may influence an individual's sexual desirability. Other interpersonal behaviors may also be related to sexual attraction. For example, interpersonal attraction theory suggests that the more a person is attracted to or likes another, the more he or she looks at that individual (e.g., Argyle & Dean, 1965; Mehrabian, 1972). Indeed, it seems commonsensical that some of the nonverbal behaviors in which we engage, including touching or eye contact, may advertise sexual interest to observers and perhaps increase our perceived sexual desirability. However, empirical research does not support this contention. For example, Suman (1990) asked participants to evaluate the sexual attractiveness of an opposite-sex confederate who either made continuous eye contact with the participants for 3 minutes or who looked away for the same duration. Sexual attractiveness ratings were unaffected by the manipulated variable.

Abbey and Melby (1986) investigated the impact of three nonverbal behaviors (interpersonal distance, eye contact, and touch) on perceptions of sexual attraction. In each study, men and women students rated photographs of heterosexual dyads whose members appeared to be studying at a table in the campus cafeteria. In the interpersonal distance study, the dyad was seated 9, 30, or 48 inches apart; in the eye contact study, the couple was either mutually gazing into each other's eyes or looking away from each other in opposite directions; in the touch study, the pair was not touching at all (no touch), their hands were near but not touching while their forearms barely touched (ambiguous touch), the male's hand was on top of the female's (male-initiated touch), the female's hand was on top of the male's (female-initiated touch), or the pair was holding hands (mutual touch). After viewing a photograph, participants rated each stimulus person on sexual traits (i.e., flirtatious, sexy, seductive, and promiscuous), and indicated how likely it was that the man was sexually attracted to the woman and vice versa, and how sexually attracted they themselves were to the opposite-sex stimulus person. Contrary to the authors' expectations, these ratings were not influenced by interpersonal distance or eye contact. The only significant result was a main effect for touch; specifically, the man and woman depicted in the photographs were perceived as more likely to be sexually attracted to each other in the mutual touch, male-initiated touch, and female-initiated touch conditions than in the no-touch or ambiguous-touch conditions. Although touch, like interpersonal distance and eye contact, did not affect observers' own sexual attraction to the opposite-sex stimulus person, this particular behavioral cue does appear to be used when making inferences about other people's feelings of sexual interest or desire.

Novelty

An individual's personal attributes and behavior may determine, in part, his or her sexual desirability. However, after a steady diet of even the most beautiful, socially successful, interpersonally warm, and provocative partners, we may find ourselves craving sexual novelty and seeking a new object for our desire. The "Coolidge effect" refers to the restoration of mating behavior in males (and, it is presumed, females) who have reached sexual satiation with one partner and who subsequently are given the opportunity to engage in sexual activity with a new partner. As noted by Bermant (1976), the term originated in a fable about former United States President Calvin Coolidge:

One day President and Mrs. Coolidge were visiting a government farm. Soon after their arrival they were taken off on separate tours.

When Mrs. Coolidge passed the chicken pens she paused to ask the man in charge if the rooster copulates more than once each day. "Dozens of times" was the reply. "Please tell that to the President," Mrs. Coolidge requested. When the President passed the pens and was told about the rooster, he asked "Same hen every time?" "Oh no, Mr. President, a different one each time." The President nodded slowly, then said "Tell that to Mrs. Coolidge." (Bermant, 1976, pp. 76-77).

It is the rooster's virility, his capacity for multiple sexual contacts in a short period of time, that captures Mrs. Coolidge's attention; it is the variety of hens simultaneously available to the rooster that the president notices. Neither one of them specifically mentions or discusses the reinitiation of sexual activity in satiated roosters; thus, the Coolidge fable does not actually illustrate the so-called Coolidge effect!

Research on this effect has been conducted almost exclusively on the sexual behavior of nonhuman male animals (for a review, see Dewsbury, 1981); it is possible, however, that the Coolidge effect may also occur with respect to sexual desire in human males and females. For example, married men and women who participated in Buunk's (1984) study indicated the extent to which nine possible reasons had played a role in their own and their spouses' engagement in an extramarital sexual relationship. A need for sexual variety was cited as a reason for their spouses' infidelity by 70% of the participants, and although the author does not report the percentage who viewed novelty as a cause of their own extramarital sexual involvement, he does note that there was no significant difference between the mean novelty rating for the partners' and perceivers' behavior.

Similar results have been reported by Regan and Dreyer (in press), who examined young adults' reasons for engaging in one-night stands, "flings," and other types of casual sexual activity. One of the most frequently cited motives for casual sex was to fill a need for sexual experimentation and exploration. For example, one woman noted that casual sex "made me feel free and liberated. . . . I just needed to feel like I could explore sexually, without any ties and obligations." Echoing these sentiments, a male participant stated that he has casual sex so that "I can sexually experiment and satisfy my curiosity about what it's like to be with different people."

These studies, like the research on animals, focus on sexual behavior rather than desire per se; nonetheless, they suggest that novelty may be one factor that whets sexual appetites.

Pheromones

Interest in the influence of pheromones—chemical secretions that elicit unlearned behavioral or developmental responses from others (Karlson & Lüscher, 1959)—on human sexual behavior has increased in recent years. Indeed, four lines of evidence seem to provide support for the speculation that a person's scent or odor may stimulate sexual desire: (a) Pheromones regulate sexual behavior in many nonhuman mammalian species (Azar, 1998; Berliner, Jennings-White, & Lavker, 1991; Cohn, 1994); (b) compounds that have pheromonal properties in pigs (i.e., androstenol and androstenone) are found in the urine and sweat of men and, to a lesser extent, women (Brooksbank, Brown, & Gustafsson, 1974; for a review see Gower & Ruparelia, 1993); (c) human infants, children, and adults are able to discriminate between other individuals on the basis of olfactory cues (e.g., Cernoch & Porter, 1985; Macfarlane, 1975; Wallace, 1977); and (d) the human nasal cavity may contain a functional (i.e., nonvestigial) vomeronasal organ—a structure that, in nonhuman animals, contains pheromone receptors (e.g., Garcia-Velasco & Mondragon, 1991; Monti-Block & Grosser, 1991; Stensaas, Lavker, Monti-Bloch, Grosser, & Berliner, 1991).

The proliferation of fragrances with names such as "Sex Appeal," "Aphrodisia," "Allure," and "Pheromone" reveals that the perfume industry, at least, subscribes to the notion that pheromones—*nonhuman* pheromones, that is—are capable of stimulating human sexual desire. One group of researchers identified 400 fragrances for women and 350 fragrances for men that contained pheromones (or their synthetic equivalents) from a variety of mammals, including the musk deer, civet cat, beaver, and pig (Berliner et al., 1991). There is little evidence, however, that these substances actually influence human sexual responses. For example, an early study revealed that exposure to the pig pheromone androstenol over a 1-month period did not significantly influence women's self-reported feelings of "sexiness" (Benton, 1982; also see Benton & Wastell, 1986), and another study found that men and women who interacted with an opposite-sex person wearing androstenol did not find that person to be more physically attractive than one wearing a synthetic musk fragrance or no applied odor (Black & Biron, 1982). In addition, at least one research team has found that women report feeling *less* sexy after exposure to androstenone than when exposed to no odor, a pleasant fruity odor, or an unpleasant fecal odor (Filsinger, Braun, Monte, & Linder, 1984).

Pheromones are species specific. Thus, it is hardly surprising that exposure to nonhuman pheromones does not directly influence sexual attraction in humans. However, it is possible that these substances have an indirect effect on desire; that is, a scent or odor may elicit a pleasant emotional response which, in turn, may increase the likelihood or intensity of sexual interest. In addition, it is likely that a particular scent or odor that has been paired repeatedly with a sex partner or with sexual activity (e.g., a specific brand of cologne or perfume) may come to produce a *learned* desire response. Of course, these types of elicited or learned responses do not constitute a true pheromone reaction.

Some research suggests that a human pheromone or "odor lure" (H. Fisher, 1992) in fact may exist. For example, both men and women have odor-producing apocrine glands in the underarm, nipple, and genital areas (Cohn, 1994). These glands become active at puberty, and their secretions may influence some aspects of reproductive physiology. For instance, the menstrual cycles of women who engage in heterosexual sexual activity on a regular basis are more regular than the menstrual cycles of women who do not engage in regular sexual activity, perhaps due to their more frequent exposure to male apocrine gland secretions (e.g., Cutler, Preti, Huggins, Erickson, & Garcia, 1985; also see Cutler et al., 1986). Whether the apocrine glands influence other reproductive or sexual responses has yet to be determined.

Other researchers posit that dead skin cells (desquamating horny cells) and the sebum (secretions) from the mouth and lips may also possess pheromonal properties (e.g., Berliner et al., 1991; Nicholson, 1984). For example, Berliner and colleagues (1991) argue that skin cells may produce pheromones and/or process pheromone precursors supplied by the blood. They suggest that these pheromones or pheromone precursors subsequently are stored within the cells, incorporated into cellular structures, or secreted into intercellular material and then are released when the skin cells or the intercellular material is sloughed off into the environment.

As the aforementioned discussion indicates, researchers are making concerted efforts to identify the chemical and biochemical structure of potential pheromones, the mechanism of pheromone communication between individuals, and the possible impact of pheromones on human emotional responses and social behavior. To date, however, the evidence for a human pheromone that influences sexual attraction remains merely speculative.

❧ The Physical Surround (Causes Located in the Physical Environment)

A growing body of research exists with respect to the influence of personal factors (e.g., hormones, beliefs) and partner characteristics (e.g., appearance) on sexual desire. Because sexual desire always occurs within a particular physical environment, it is likely that external conditions also affect this particular sexual experience. Indeed, men and women apparently recognize the potential impact of physical environmental factors on sexual desire. Soft music, candlelit dinners, and erotic or sexually suggestive scenery commonly are assumed to set the stage for romantic interludes and sexual encounters and are manipulated accordingly by individuals eager to heighten or lower the sexual temperature of the relationship. However, despite the prominent role given these factors in virtually every cinematic (and real-world) seduction scene, little research has been conducted on whether such environmental properties actually incite or increase sexual desire.

At least one study suggests that exposure to some external factors—in particular, to erotic or pornographic media—may *decrease* the perceived sexual desirability of an available sexual partner. In the first of two studies, Kenrick, Gutierres, and Goldberg (1989) asked men and women to view slides of very attractive nude women pictured in the magazines *Playboy* and *Penthouse*, average-looking nude women, or abstract art slides. All participants then viewed a slide of an average attractive nude woman and provided ratings of her sexual attractiveness, how attractive she was to men, and how desirable they imagined that men would find her as a date. These three items were combined to form a global sexual attractiveness scale. For both men and women, exposure to the attractive centerfolds (but not the abstract art or average-looking nude women) resulted in lowered judgments of the target woman's sexual attractiveness. The authors conducted a second study to examine whether the same contrast effect would occur with judgments made about an actual relationship partner. Specifically, men and women viewed either nude opposite-sex centerfolds or abstract art slides and then rated their marital or cohabiting partner on the same sexual attractiveness measures used in the first study, which again were aggregated to form one independent variable. Men's ratings of their partners' sexual attractiveness were significantly adversely affected by prior exposure to erotica (i.e., men who were exposed to nude centerfolds rated their partners as significantly less sexually attractive than men who viewed abstract art). However, women's ratings of their partners' sexual attractiveness were not influenced by the type of prior stimuli. The authors remind readers that the physical attractiveness of the centerfold stimuli, not their erotic nature, is responsible for the contrast effect obtained. Whatever the case, exposure to erotic or pornographic media (or for that matter, to any media that focuses on unusually attractive people) may create unrealistic expectations about what an average person looks like naked; this, in turn, may result in decreased sexual desire for "real-life" partners.

Research on the correlates of casual sexual encounters between strangers (i.e., one-night stands) suggests that other physical settings or circumstances may *increase* sexual desire or at least the willingness to behave in accordance with one's sexual desires (e.g., Eiser & Ford, 1995; Herold & Mewhinney, 1993; Regan & Dreyer, in press). For example, Regan and Dreyer (in press) reported that 17% of their sample of participants cited such aspects of the physical environment as a dark, private setting, a party situation, vacation or travel, and the availability of contraception as reasons for their short-term encounters.

The Relationship

In the previous chapter, we considered the ways in which emotions experienced within a relationship and/or directed toward a partner may influence the experience of sexual desire. For example, anger or other negative affects stemming from interpersonal conflict may suppress sexual desire (e.g., Arnett et al., 1986; Kaplan, 1979; Trudel, 1991), whereas anxiety about how a partner will respond to one's sexual overtures may increase sexual desire (e.g., Hatfield & Rapson, 1987).

Indeed, as a growing number of couples enter sex therapy with the aim of increasing one partner's (or both partners') diminished sexual desire, it has become clear that the experience of sexual desire is intricately connected to the quality of the relationship between individuals and other interpersonal phenomena. For example, "emotional conflict with partner" was cited as the most common cause of inhibited sexual desire among married men and women in a survey of 400 physicians (Pietropinto, 1986), and many clinicians now focus on the dynamics of the couple's relationship in seeking to understand and treat desire disorders (e.g., Fish et al., 1984; Kaplan, 1979; Leiblum & Rosen, 1988; Regas & Sprenkle, 1984; Talmadge & Talmadge, 1986; Trudel, 1991).

At least two studies provide empirical support for the hypothesis that sexual desire disorders signal the existence of other problems in a couple's relationship. Stuart et al. (1987) administered the Dyadic Adjustment Scale (DAS) to 59 married women who were diagnosed with inhibited sexual desire (ISD) and to 31 married women who reported normal sexual desire. The women in the ISD group scored significantly lower in marital adjustment on all four subscales (consensus, satisfaction, cohesion, and affection) and on the total scale than did women in the non-ISD group, and the spouses of women in the ISD group also reported significantly lower overall satisfactory adjustment in their marriage and lower levels of affection than the spouses of non-ISD women. Stuart and colleagues also asked respondents to rate their subjective feelings about the quality of their relationship with their spouse. ISD women were significantly less satisfied with the way in which interpersonal conflict was resolved and with their own and their spouses' listening ability, and they reported experiencing significantly lower levels of emotional closeness, romantic feelings, and love toward their spouses.

A longitudinal study conducted by Hallstrom and Samuelsson (1990) also suggests that relationship properties may affect the experience of sexual desire. The authors interviewed 497 women who were married or cohabiting with a male partner, on two occasions 6 years apart. Women were asked about the present degree of their sexual desire (i.e., whether they perceived it as strong, moderate, weak, or absent), and to report whether they received insufficient emotional support from their spouse (yes/no) and lacked a confiding relationship with him (yes/no). Although causality cannot be determined from this correlational design, a *decrease* in self-reported sexual desire over time was predicted by a perceived lack of a confiding relationship with and insufficient support from the spouse at the first interview. It does appear that sexual desire is affected by interpersonal factors.

❧ Conclusions

This chapter reviewed empirical research conducted on various external causes of sexual desire. We considered the ways in which sexual desire is influenced by partner characteristics, by factors associated with the physical environment, and by the relationship with the sexual partner. It was clear from the latter review that sentiment for the partner is a particularly potent correlate of sexual desire. In the next chapter, we explore the sentiment believed to be the most closely associated with sexual desire—namely, romantic or passionate love.

7

Sexual Desire and
Romantic Love

As we have noted in several places in this book, anecdotal clinical evidence as well as a growing number of empirical investigations suggest that the waxing and waning of sexual desire in a relationship reflects how well a couple is functioning in other, nonsexual relational areas. Some clinicians, in fact, argue that sexual desire is caused by feelings of romantic love. For example, Kaplan (1979) proposes that "love is the best aphrodisiac discovered so far" (p. 61), a belief echoed by Levine (1982). Ironically, social psychologists are now exploring the possibility that sexual desire actually causes romantic love (or that it is a necessary although not sufficient condition for the experience of romantic love). In this chapter, we consider what theorists from a number of disciplines have had to say about the association between romantic love (also called passionate love or erotic love) and sexual desire, we present a historical overview of social psychological discourse on the nature of romantic love and its relation to sexual desire, and we review indirect and direct empirical evidence about the link, if any, between these two fundamentally important human life experiences.

☙ Sexual Desire and Romantic Love: Early Theoretical Discourse

The link of sexual desire with romantic love has been a pervasive theme in a variety of disciplines, including sexual pathology and medicine, psychoanalysis, and existential philosophy and religious theology. As early as 1886, the German physician Richard von Krafft-Ebing, whose pioneering observations of sexually disturbed individuals provided the foundation for modern sexual pathology, distinguished fleeting, "purely sensual love" (1886/1945, p. 12) or romantic love from "true" love, "sentimental" love, "platonic" love, and "friendship." In discussing the sexual nature of this type of love he argued the following:

> Since love implies the presence of sexual desire it can only exist between persons of different sex capable of sexual intercourse. When these conditions are wanting or destroyed it is replaced by friendship. (p. 13)

This view may seem antiquated—it is now acknowledged, for example, that romantic love and sexual desire can and do occur within same-sex relationships—but Krafft-Ebing's fundamental assertion that romantic love consists of friendship ignited by the spark of sexual desire has been echoed by philosophers and theorists throughout the past century.

Unlike Krafft-Ebing, the English physician and sexologist Havelock Ellis (1859-1939) focused primarily on nonpathological sexual phenomena and viewed male and female sexuality as normal aspects of human development and function. However, Krafft-Ebing's notion of romantic love as a mixture of sexual desire and affection is paramount in Ellis' many-volumed *Studies in the Psychology of Sex* (1897-1928), a substantial portion of which is devoted to an examination of the relationship between love, sex, and marriage. His purpose was neither to develop a typology of love nor to discuss romance or romantic love per se; nonetheless, Ellis concluded that the love that frequently occurs between men and women is best viewed as a mixture of lust, or the physiological sexual impulse, and friendship, which includes other impulses of a more tender, affectionate nature (see, for example, 1933/1963, p. 234). Although he viewed romantic love as more than just sexual desire and believed that sexual feelings or behaviors that occurred in the absence of affection were simple manifestations of lust, Ellis obviously found sexual desire to be an important part of romantic love.

Sigmund Freud, one of Havelock Ellis' contemporaries and the founder of psychoanalytic theory, became interested in the relation of sex to personality development and to human life experiences such as romantic love when he discovered that many of his patients' hysterical and neurotic symptoms had origins of a decidedly sexual nature, often stemming from experiences that had occurred during childhood and adolescence. Like Havelock Ellis, this noted neurologist and psychiatrist also associated romantic love or the "love-impulse" (Freud, 1908/1963a, p. 34) with sexual desire. According to psychoanalytic theory, romantic love is produced when the sexual instinct inherent within all individuals manifests itself as a psychical attachment to the current love object. In other words, romantic love stems from a primitive, sexual urge and represents the suppression or sublimation of this sexual instinct. Viewed in this manner, love becomes essentially the same as sexual attraction or desire, reflected or interpreted psychically. Interestingly, Freud later modified his view of romantic love to include a more affiliative component, concluding in 1912 that "to ensure a fully normal attitude in love, two currents of feeling have to unite—we may describe them as the tender, affectionate feelings and the sensual feelings" (1912/1963c, p. 59).

The view that romantic love is primarily the product of sexual desire is echoed by psychotherapist Albert Ellis in his classic (1954) work, *The American Sexual Tragedy*. Following a thorough examination of the popular mass media of the time as well as a diverting excursion through the personal experiences of colleagues and friends and the free associations and dreams of his clients, he concluded that

> all love is not, of course, romantic love. Love itself consists of any kind of more or less intense emotional attraction to or involvement with another. It includes many different types and degrees of affection, such as conjugal love, parental love, familial love, religious love, love of humanity, love of animals, love of things, self-love, sexual love, obsessive-compulsive love, etc. Although *romantic* has become, in our day, virtually a synonym for *loving*, romantic love is actually a special type of love, and has several distinguishing features. (p. 101)

According to Ellis, one of those distinguishing features is that romantic love is in fact derived almost exclusively from (thwarted) sexual desire produced by the dynamics of the couple relationship:

> Romantic love, again, is largely based on the sexual teasing and blocking of modern courtship. Its very intensity, to a large part, grows out of the generous promises combined with the niggardly actualities of sex fulfillment which exist during the courtship stages. (p. 113)

The heady, perfectionistic, idealized experience of romantic love is far more fleeting than the calm, steady, enduring, domestic love that Ellis believed to be characteristic of well-adjusted marital relationships. Indeed, the former can survive only as long as sexual desire is permitted no outlet. Once the urgent pangs of desire are sated via intercourse, romantic love will inevitably perish—"sexual and marital consummation indubitably, in the vast majority of instances, maims, bloodies, and finally kills romanticism until it is deader than—well, yesterday's romance" (p. 116). Romance, then, is said to rarely survive beyond the opening sexual maneuvers of the marriage campaign.

Noted love theorist and psychotherapist Theodor Reik would have agreed that romantic love is short-lived, but he would have taken issue with the amount of notice given to sexual desire in traditional psychoanalytic discourse. According to Reik (1944, 1945), we fall out of love *not* when we no longer sexually desire our beloved, but when the pedestal on which we have placed that individual inevitably cracks and tumbles to the ground as the result of the numerous disappointments that eventually taint any romantic relationship. Reik theorized that love is much more than the "sex in disguise" (1944, p. 15) or "washed-out sexual urge" (1945, p. 18) so dear to Freudian theory, or the thwarted sexual desire posited by Albert Ellis:

> That love between men and women is in most cases accompanied by sexual desire has nothing to do with the nature of love itself. A chemist who examines the fusion of two materials will not assert that they are the same or have the same properties. Their affinity does not mean that they are identical or that their formulas are the same. (Reik, 1945, pp. 101-102)

However, the fact that love and sexual desire are fundamentally different phenomena does not mean that the presence of sexual desire is antithetical to that of romantic love. Although Reik (1944) theorized that the two are not one and the same, he conceded that they frequently coexist and thus may be experienced as one emotion. In fact, he wrote that love stems from the fusion of three distinct drives—sexual desire or the sex urge, the will to conquer, and affection. It is not clear whether this love of which Reik wrote in 1944 is in fact romantic love or rather some more global construct, but he argued in his 1945 work, *Psychology of Sex Relations*, that romantic or passionate love was born at a time in our ancestral past when love finally advanced into the realm of sexual expression and that it can therefore be understood as a combination of sexual and tender feelings. Thus, although sexual desire does not constitute romantic love, it nonetheless is intricately linked to that phenomenon.

Similarly, although existential psychologist Erich Fromm (1956) also took issue with the original Freudian notion that romantic love is exclusively the expression (or, more accurately, the suppression) of the sexual instinct, sexual desire remains firmly associated with romantic love in his theoretical musings. According to Fromm's typology, erotic love is an exclusive form of love that represents "the craving for complete fusion, for union with one other person" (pp. 52-53). Unlike brotherly love (love among equals) and motherly love (love for the helpless), this form of love is related to phenomena such as sexual satisfaction and desire. For example, he argued that sexual happiness is the inevitable result of love and that sexual desire is a manifestation of the need for love and union. However, Fromm, like Reik, believed that erotic love is more than the sum of these sexual phenomena: "Love can inspire the wish for sexual union; in this case the physical relationship is lacking in greediness, in a wish to conquer or to be conquered, but is blended with tenderness" (Fromm, 1956, p. 54). Because sexual desire is so closely associated with romantic love, Fromm cautioned that many individuals are easily misled to conclude that they are in love with each other when in fact they simply desire one another sexually. We are only "in love" with the objects of our sexual desire when they are also the objects of our affection.

This theme is echoed by religious theoretician C. S. Lewis (1960) in his delightful though somewhat tortuous work *The Four Loves*. Different from Affection, Friendship, and Charity, Eros or "being in love" contains a carnal sexual element that he refers to as Venus. In addition to this sexual desire component, erotic love invariably is fused with affectionate love (the warm, comfortable, diffuse love such as that seen between parents and children). Perhaps as the result of the addition of these tender feelings, the element of sexual desire that is so strongly a part of erotic love develops into something that is more than an explicitly sexual appetite, eventually becoming an individualized sexual desire directed solely toward the beloved. Essentially, the short-lived, transitory experience of erotic love is a fusion of affection and sexual desire.

In sum, although each of the aforementioned individuals argues vociferously in support of his own pet theory, all conceive of romantic love as an intense, fleeting state created and inspired by the fusion of sexual desire with a nonsexual, affectionate feeling or instinct. Some emphasize the latter component more than others; however, in every instance sexual desire is posited as the essential ingredient for romantic love. In addition, this sexual desire component is crucial to the maintenance of romantic love. If at any time sexual desire disappears, a person is no longer said to be in a state of romantic love. Sated desire leaves lovers at worst disillusioned and disappointed, at best ruefully wondering where the "spark" in their relationship has gone and regretfully reminiscing about the good old days.

❧ Social Psychology and Romantic Love

As illustrated by the preceding review, romantic or passionate love has been the subject of much speculation throughout the past hundred years or so. No discipline has evinced as much interest in or contributed as much theory and research on romantic love as has social psychology. Although social psychologists have proposed numerous types or varieties of love (e.g., Hendrick & Hendrick, 1992; Sternberg & Barnes, 1988), romantic love has assumed special importance in social psychological research and theory for a number of reasons: Romantic love generally is sought after by individuals and exalted in Western culture; romantic love has become the *sine qua non* of the marriage contract; and the absence of romantic love may be a factor in relationship dissolution (e.g., Berscheid, 1985; Burgess & Wallin, 1953; Goode, 1959; Kazak & Reppucci, 1980; Kephart, 1967; Simpson, Campbell, & Berscheid, 1986; Spaulding, 1971).[1]

Sexless Romantic Love

Interestingly, social psychological conceptualizations of romantic love have been sexless until relatively recently. As noted by Berscheid and Walster (1974a), for many years, social psychologists interested in romantic love contented themselves with vague abstractions and generalizations gleaned from the vast literature on interpersonal attraction. Love, it was assumed, was nothing more than a form of intense interpersonal attraction, a sort of liking run wild. The determinants of romantic love were therefore thought to be simply more intense versions of the antecedents of liking, and the principles of reinforcement that neatly explain why we prefer or like certain persons over others were assumed to explain the reasons we fall in love with one individual and not another.

Because sexuality was not hypothesized to be one of the major determinants of liking, those social psychologists who used the conceptual framework associated with liking and interpersonal attraction presented a view of romantic love that was remarkably devoid of sex. For example, noted attraction and love researcher Rubin (e.g., 1970, 1973) was one of the first individuals to attempt to operationalize and empirically distinguish between romantic love and related phenomena such as liking, or interpersonal attraction, and the love between children and parents, an individual and God, and close friends. He argued that romantic love, defined as "love between unmarried opposite-sex peers, of the sort which could possibly lead to marriage" (1970, p. 266), is associated with a physical or emotional need, "a passionate desire to possess and to be fulfilled by another person" (1973, p. 213). However, he chose to interpret this "love-need" as a nonsexual attachment similar to the bonds formed between infants and their parents; it is not surprising, then, that the 13 items on Rubin's romantic love scale reflect affiliative and dependent needs, the predisposition to help the partner, and nonsexual feelings of exclusiveness, absorption, and possessiveness. None of the scale items could be considered even remotely sexual—the most sexually charged item states, "When I am with _____, I spend a good deal of time just looking at him (her)" (1970, p. 267). Rubin's romantic love scale is moderately correlated with the scale he developed to measure liking (e.g., Mathes, 1984; Rubin, 1970), suggesting that the two may reflect essentially the same nonsexual, affection-based construct.

Other researchers and theorists concerned with romantic love have similarly ignored or downplayed the sexual aspects of the phenomenon in their conceptualizations and measures. For example, the questionnaire designed by Dion and Dion (e.g., 1973) to assess the "intense, mysterious, and volatile" (p. 51) phenomenon of romantic love is noticeably sexless. This measure included a list of stereotypic romantic love "symptoms" such as feelings of euphoria and depression, agitation and restlessness, daydreaming, sleep difficulties, and decreased ability to concentrate. Items designed to assess attitudes toward romantic love are similarly lacking in sexual content, and the only seemingly sexual dimensions included on a series of romantic love adjective rating scales are "sensual-intellectual" and "spiritual-physical" (p. 54).

Driscoll, Davis, and Lipetz (1972) distinguished between romantic love, defined as "a distinct form of interpersonal attraction that occurs between opposite-sex partners under specifiable social conditions" (p. 1), and what they called "conjugal love," or the trusting, loyal, appreciative love found between mature adults and close friends. Interestingly, these authors expanded their conceptualization of romantic love to include feelings of passion and physical attraction, but their four-item love scale assesses only general feelings of love, caring, need, and the importance of the relationship. No items related to sexual feelings toward the partner are included.

Similarly, items included on Bardis's (1971) "erotometer" were ostensibly selected to represent 18 aspects of "heterosexual love" (p. 71). Like Driscoll et al. (1972), Bardis clearly associated the physical aspect of this variety of love with the sexual elements of the love relationship (see p. 72) and thus at least tipped his theoretical hat to the connection between romantic love and sex. However, an examination of the 50 items composing his scale reveals nothing explicitly or implicitly sexual in nature or tone (the most sexual items read "Longing to do things together" and "Enjoying just being together").

More recently, Brehm (1988) has argued that passionate (romantic) love is an intense and not particularly sexual experience that represents the combination of imagination and emotion and that serves to motivate human beings to construct a vision of a better world. Critical aspects or consequences of passionate love include the emotional experiences of joy, frustration, aridity (feelings of being dry, barren, and unresponsive that signal emotional exhaustion), and terror; the motivation to act in ways that promote closeness to the beloved; and detachment from other people and things that are not directly related to the beloved. Although Brehm recognizes that romantic or passionate love may have sexual consequences, she nonetheless concludes that sex has very little to do with the experience:

> It may seem strange that, in this discussion of passionate love, I have given so little attention to sex. Passionate love does, of course, often focus on a potential or existing sexual partner, and desired or actual sexual activity with that partner can be a major source of heightened emotional experience. I do not, however, regard sexuality as a necessary component of passionate love . . . it is a serious mistake to regard all forms of passionate love as essentially sexual in origin or purpose. Just as one can have a highly active sexual life without a trace of passionate love, so one can be passionately in love independent of one's sexual drives. (p. 257)

Certainly it is possible to feel desire for, become aroused by, and engage in sexual activities with individuals for whom we feel little or no romantic love; however, the assertion that romantic love exists independently of sexuality has come under attack in recent years.

The Sexualization of Romantic Love

Social psychological theorists gradually have recognized that sexual phenomena ought to be included in conceptualizations and measures of romantic love. For example, Elaine Hatfield (then Walster) and Ellen Berscheid (1971; Berscheid & Walster, 1974a)—among the first contemporary researchers to conduct a dialogue on the nature of romantic love—conceptualized passionate or romantic love as an exotic variety of interpersonal attraction. According to these researchers, this fragile, temporary, intense phenomenon blossoms only when an individual is extremely aroused physiologically and when situational or contextual cues indicate that "passionate love" is the appropriate label for that arousal. Emotional experiences such as fear, rejection, frustration, hatred, excitement, and sexual gratification that are all associated with physiological arousal can be instrumental in producing and enhancing passionate feelings. Berscheid and Walster quite explicitly provide a place for such sexual phenomena as arousal and gratification in their elegant and thorough discussion: They posit, for example, that the inhibition of sexual satisfaction and the sexual challenge provided by "hard to get" men and women will increase the romantic feelings of erstwhile admirers.

A good portion of Hatfield and Walster's (1978) discussion of passionate love stems from earlier work conducted with Berscheid and similarly emphasizes the sexual aspects of romantic love. For example, we learn that passionate love consists of a wild confusion of tender, sexual, painful, anxious, altruistic, and jealous feelings and that feelings of passion and romance are promoted by physiologically arousing states such as anxiety, anger, fear, loneliness, and sexual deprivation that often heighten sexual attraction and subjective and physiological sexual arousal (also see Hatfield, 1988). In contrast to the affectionate, companionate love often seen between old friends or long-married couples, passionate love is described as a short-lived state, dying quickly once sexual aims are satisfied and the novelty of sexual activity with the heretofore unattainable object inevitably degenerates into routine sex with a no longer exciting partner.

Other authors also recognize that romantic love contains a sexual element. For example, Lee (e.g., 1973, 1988) devoted considerable energy to an examination of different types of love, in the process developing a novel approach in which different styles of loving are likened to primary or secondary colors (hence the title of his 1973 book, *Colours of Love*). Eros, one of the primary colors or styles of loving, is an intensely emotional experience similar to the passionate love described by Berscheid, Hatfield, and Walster. According to Lee, the erotic lover is "turned on" by a particular physical type, is prone to fall instantly and completely in love with a stranger ("love at first sight"), rapidly becomes preoccupied with pleasant thoughts about that individual, experiences an intense need for daily contact with the beloved, and wishes the relationship to remain exclusive. Like passionate love, erotic love has a sexual component; for example, not only does the erotic style of loving always begin with a strong physical attraction, but the erotic lover always seeks some form of sexual involvement early in the relationship. Indeed, in profiling the typical erotic lover, Lee (1988) writes that he or she is "eager to get to know the beloved quickly, intensely—and undressed" (p. 50).

Originally fascinated by the oftentimes devastating emotional aftermath of broken love relationships, Tennov (1979) set out to characterize the agony and ecstasy of the individual experience of being "in love." In her fascinating (1979) book, *Love and Limerence*, she coined the now famous term *limerence* to describe the state of what others have called erotic, passionate, or romantic love. Limerence is an intense mental state or cognitive obsession characterized by persistent, intrusive thought about the object of passionate desire (called the limerent object or "LO"): acute longing for reciprocation; mood fluctuations; intense awareness of the LO's actions; fear of rejection; shyness; physical reactions (i.e., "heartache"); emotional highs and lows depending on the LO's perceived reciprocity; and idealization of the LO's positive qualities. Limerence is not the same as sexual attraction, and sexual activity is not enough to satisfy the limerent need. However, Tennov strongly believed that sexual feelings are a necessary part of the limerent experience:

> I am inclined toward the generalization that sexual attraction is an essential component of limerence. This sexual feeling may be combined with shyness, impotence or some form of sexual dysfunction or disinclination, or with some social unsuitability. But LO, in order to become LO, must stand in relation to the limerent as one for whom

the limerent is a potential sex partner. Sexual attraction is not "enough," to be sure. Selection standards for limerence are, according to informants, not identical to those by which "mere" sexual partners are evaluated, and sex is seldom the main focus of limerence. Either the potential for sexual mating is felt to be there, however, or the state described is not limerence. (pp. 24-25)

Limerence generally fades after a period of time, although it may be supplanted by a more genuine form of love based on support, care, and concern.

Intimacy, decision/commitment, and passion form the vertices of Sternberg's more recent triangular theory of love (e.g., 1986, 1988). The intimacy component refers to feelings of warmth, closeness, and connection in the love relationship; the decision/commitment component represents both the short-term decision that one individual loves another and the longer-term commitment to maintain that love; and the passion component refers to "the drives that lead to romance, physical attraction, sexual consummation, and the like in a loving relationship" (1988, p. 120). According to Sternberg, all forms of love (specifically, eight) can be conceptualized as combinations of one or more of these components. For example, romantic love derives from the combination of the intimacy and passion components of love and thus can be viewed as liking or friendship with the added spice of physical or sexual attraction.

Similarly, Branden's (1988) conceptualization of romantic love— defined as a "passionate spiritual-emotional-sexual attachment between two people that reflects a high regard for the value of each other's person" (p. 220)—contains sexual elements. Arguing that romantic love allows people to satisfy the psychological need for sexual fulfillment, he notes that individuals who are in love not only view the loved one as critically important to their sexual happiness, but they tend to express their love physically, via sexual encounters. According to Branden, a relationship cannot be viewed as romantic if it lacks a strong sexual attraction.

Like Sternberg and Branden, Murstein's (1988) conceptualization of romantic love also includes an emphasis on physical passion. This theorist argues that there are three stages of love: (a) passionate love or physical attraction, which involves intense arousal and has a strong sexual base; (b) romantic love, which resembles passionate love but is more focused on the idealization of the beloved; and (c) conjugal or companionate love, which is characterized by liking and trust. Although Murstein contends that romantic love is a less explicitly sexual experience than passionate love, he maintains that it does have a physical or sexual element.

Shaver, Hazan, and colleagues conceptualize romantic love as a biological process that has been designed by evolution to facilitate the attachment between adult sexual partners (e.g., Hazan & Shaver, 1987; Shaver & Hazan, 1988; Shaver, Hazan, & Bradshaw, 1988). These researchers note that the key features of infant-caregiver attachment are remarkably similar to those of adult romantic love: For example, an infant seeks to maintain proximity and contact with his or her primary caregiver by engaging in behaviors such as holding, touching, kissing, clinging, and smiling. Romantic lovers also seek to spend time with and maintain physical contact with the loved object; specifically, they hold, touch, caress, kiss, make love with, and smile at the partner. However, adult romantic love differs from infant-caregiver attachment in two important ways: Not only do adult romantic partners engage in reciprocal caregiving, but sexual attraction and sexual behavior are an important part of romantic love. Thus, Shaver and colleagues argue that adult romantic love involves the integration of three independent behavioral systems: attachment, reciprocal caregiving, and sexuality (described as an innate system consisting of a cycle of desire and arousal followed by sexual behavior and orgasm). Although different romantic love relationships involve different mixtures of these components (e.g., one-sided "crushes" and nonsexual romantic relationships), these researchers contend that prototypical adult romantic love contains all three elements.

Buss (e.g., 1988) also takes an evolutionary approach to romantic love, arguing that the key consequences of this phenomenon center around reproduction. Specifically, he hypothesizes that the acts or behaviors that fall in the category of "love" have evolved to achieve proximate goals such as sexual intimacy and reproduction, among others. In fact, Buss proposes that sexual intimacy is the *sine qua non* of "heterosexual love," described as the state of being "in love." Love acts of sexual intimacy—which include engaging in sexual intercourse, losing one's virginity to the loved one, and being "sexually open" with one's partner—serve to seal the bond between lovers and may result in conception.

The increasing attention given to sexual phenomena in theoretical discourses on the nature of romantic love has gradually permeated the empirical literature in social psychology. For example, Critelli, Myers, and Loos (1986) created their measure of romantic love by supplementing existing love scales constructed by Rubin (1970) and Driscoll et al. (1972) with items designed to reflect feelings of sexual arousal, physiological arousal, passion, excitement, romance, and physical attraction; Pam, Plutchik, and Conte (1975) included items related to the physical and sexual attractiveness of the romantic partner in their measure of "being in love" (p. 83); and Swensen and colleagues (Swensen, 1961; Swensen & Gilner, 1963) placed a physical expression category (containing items concerned with sexual behaviors such as hugging, kissing, "necking," "petting," and sexual relations) among the other varieties of love expression assessed by their particular measure. Like Critelli et al. (1986), Hendrick and Hendrick (1986) recognized that erotic love contains elements of "strong physical preferences, early attraction, and intensity of emotion" (p. 400). Of the seven items designed to assess this particular love style, three directly relate to sexual attraction, behavior, and satisfaction. Specifically, the final version of the scale contains items assessing the extent to which the participant believes that he or she and the partner experienced immediate mutual attraction, have the right physical "chemistry" between them, and engage in very intense and satisfying lovemaking. Subsequent revisions of the erotic love measure have continued to emphasize the sexual nature of this type of love (Hendrick, Hendrick, & Dicke, 1998).

All of the aforementioned theorists and researchers seem to agree that romantic love contains a sexual component that differentiates it from other types or varieties of love. Where they lack consensus is in the specification of the precise nature of that sexual component. The existing theoretical statements and empirical measures contain an interesting mixture of sexual phenomena, including *physical and/or sexual attraction* (e.g., Critelli et al., 1986; Hatfield, 1988; Hatfield & Walster, 1978; Hendrick & Hendrick, 1986; Lee, 1973; Pam et al., 1975; Shaver & Hazan, 1988; Sternberg, 1988; Tennov, 1979), *sexual excitement* (e.g., Critelli et al., 1986; Hatfield & Walster, 1978), *physiological and/or sexual arousal* (e.g., Critelli et al., 1986; Hatfield & Sprecher, 1986; Hatfield & Walster, 1978; Shaver et al., 1988), *sexual deprivation* (e.g., Hatfield & Walster, 1978), *sexual satisfaction and/or gratification* (e.g., Berscheid & Walster, 1974a; Hendrick & Hendrick, 1986; Shaver et al., 1988; Walster & Berscheid, 1971), *sexual involvement* (e.g., Hendrick & Hendrick, 1986; Lee, 1973, 1988), and *sexual activity* (e.g., Buss, 1988; Shaver & Hazan, 1988; Swensen, 1961; Swensen & Gilner, 1963). These phenomena do not represent the same, or in some instances even similar, concepts.

In sum, social psychological conceptualizations of romantic love run the gamut from the completely asexual to the highly sexual. In addition, a wide array of sexual phenomena have been targeted as possible components of the romantic love experience by those theorists and researchers who include sexuality in their conceptualizations and measures. However, although some authors use the seemingly euphemistic terms *passion, sexual attraction,* and *sexual feelings* in their descriptions and measures of romantic love, sexual desire itself has been overlooked. For example, none of the love scales we reviewed contains items specifically designed to reflect sexual desire, nor do any theorists make explicit the relation between sexual desire and romantic love. However, as we discuss in the following section, this state of affairs is changing.

Contemporary Social Psychological Discourse

Contemporary romantic love theorists seem to have (re)discovered sexual desire. Social psychologists who prior to this time were content to view the sexual component of romantic love as an undifferentiated construct encompassing anything from sexual attraction to sexual feelings to sexual arousal to sexual activity are now beginning to call loudly and specifically for the reinstatement of sexual desire into the dialogue on the nature of romantic love. For example, Berscheid (1988) ended her comments on the state of social psychological theory and research with respect to romantic love with the following admonition:

My third, and final, conclusion (to which I've already alluded) is that the role of sexual desire and experience has been neglected in contemporary discussions of romantic love. It is all very well to look down one's nose at Sigmund Freud's cursory analysis of romantic love as repressed, suppressed, or frustrated sexual desire, but, for me at least, Freud seems to have gotten smarter as I've gotten older. And, surely, it is no accident that the wisest of the romantic love theorists, Theodore Reik, entitled his classic book *Of Love and Lust* (1941) (and not, by the way, "Of Love and Liking"). (p. 372)

Others have taken a similar stance. Hatfield and her colleagues no longer view passionate love as an amorphous amalgamation of undifferentiated "tender and sexual feelings" (Hatfield, Traupmann, & Sprecher, 1984, p. 109) but now argue that passionate love, "the desire for union with another," and sexual desire, "the desire for *sexual* union with another," have much in common and can in fact can be explained by the same paradigm (Hatfield & Rapson, 1987, p. 259). Specifically, Hatfield and Rapson (1987) believe that both passionate love and sexual desire are fueled by and thrive under the "right conditions"— in this case, a mixture of both intensely positive and intensely negative emotional experiences such as delight, security, anger, anxiety, and jealousy (see also Hatfield, 1988).

Indeed, Hatfield and Sprecher's (1986) Passionate Love Scale represents perhaps the best measure of romantic love currently available. Drawing on past theoretical conceptualizations, previously developed romantic love measures, and in-depth personal interviews, these researchers carefully crafted a series of items designed to represent the cognitive, emotional, and behavioral components of the passionate love experience. Subsequent administration and revision of this original set of items resulted in a 30-item scale that reliably discriminates between feelings of passionate versus companionate love. Of particular interest is the fact that the scale contains a number of items directly and indirectly relevant to the sexual aspect of passionate love, including the following:

3. Sometimes my body trembles with excitement at the sight of _____.

4. I take delight in studying the movements and angles of _____'s body.

11. I want _____—physically, emotionally, mentally.

13. I melt when looking deeply into _____'s eyes.

17. I sense my body responding when _____ touches me.

24. I eagerly look for signs indicating _____'s desire for me.

27. In the presence of _____, I yearn to touch and be touched.

29. I possess a powerful attraction for _____.

Items 27 and 29, and perhaps items 11 and 24, seem in particular to capture the essence of sexual desire.

Romantic love *is* different from the other types of love that have been labeled and discussed over the years, and we believe that Freud, Reik and their contemporary counterparts in the social sciences have correctly surmised wherein that difference lies: Sexual desire is a distinguishing feature and a prerequisite of the romantic love experience. The proof, however, is in the pudding. In the remainder of this chapter, then, we examine empirical evidence, some conducted by ourselves, that speaks to the question of whether sexual desire in fact is related to the experience of romantic love.

ɜ Sexual Desire and Romantic Love: Research

Indirect Empirical Evidence

Indirect empirical support for the association between sexual desire and romantic love is provided by several sources. For example, during the process of scale validation, Hatfield and Sprecher (1986) gave their Passionate Love Scale (PLS) and a battery of various other measures to students involved in dating or more serious relationships. These researchers found that scores for both men and women on the PLS scale correlated significantly with self-reported satisfaction with the sexual aspect of the current relationship, as well as with several ratings of current desire for physical interaction with the partner. Specifically, higher PLS scores were associated with an increased desire to be held by the partner, to kiss the partner, and to engage in sex with the partner. Individuals who are very passionately in love, then, experience more sexual desire for their partner than do people who are less passionately in love.

Similar results were reported earlier by Pam et al. (1975). These researchers administered their 30-item love scale to a group of unmarried male and female college students who were reportedly either in love, dating but not in love, or merely friendly with another individual of the opposite sex. Results indicated that the "in love" group and the "friendship" group scored essentially the same on the respect subscale and significantly higher than the "dating" group, implying that respect is as important an aspect of romantic relationships as it is of friendships. However, when a comparison of means was made for the physical attraction subscale (recall that this contained items assessing the perceived physical and sexual attractiveness of the partner), the "in love" group had a significantly higher mean score than either the "dating" or "friendship" group. It thus appears that the sexual desirability of the partner is a vital component of a romantic relationship.

The results of a recent study conducted by Sprecher and Regan (1998) provide additional, albeit limited, support for the hypothesized romantic love-sexual desire connection. These researchers were interested in exploring whether two types of love—passionate or romantic love and companionate love (a stable, affectionate love based on trust and friendship)—differentially are associated with a variety of interpersonal events and phenomena. A sample of 197 heterosexual couples completed the Companionate Love Scale (CLS, adapted from Rubin's, 1970, love scale) and a shortened version of Hatfield and Sprecher's (1986) PLS, as well as global, single-item measures of each love type. Couples also indicated how often they had experienced "sexual excitement" for the partner in the past month and completed a six-item sexual intimacy scale that assessed, for example, sexual satisfaction, ability to express sexual interest to the partner, and the partner's perceived interest in sex. The results revealed that both passionate and companionate love were positively correlated with these two sexuality variables. However, for both men and women, the experience of sexual excitement was more strongly correlated with passionate love scores than with companionate love scores, whereas feelings of sexual intimacy were more strongly related to companionate love scores than to passionate love scores. The researchers concluded that different aspects of sexuality may be more (or less) associated with particular types or varieties of love. Specifically, these results suggest that intense, physiological or motivational components of sexuality (e.g., sexual excitement, sexual desire) may be important features of the passionate love experience, whereas low-key, subjective sexual feelings related to closeness, warmth, satisfaction, and compatibility (i.e., sexual intimacy) are an important part of the companionate love experience.

Direct Empirical Evidence

None of the above research was specifically designed to assess the relationship between sexual desire and romantic love, and thus the results, while suggestive, provide at best only weak support for that association. However, in recent years, a growing number of researchers have attempted to explicitly examine this relationship.

We discussed some of the empirical findings of Beck and colleagues (1991) earlier in this volume. These researchers were primarily interested in various aspects of sexual desire, including the frequency with which desire is experienced by men and women and the means by which individuals gauge their level of sexual desire. However, they also examined the relation between self-reported frequency of sexual desire and romantic love. Students completed a sexual desire questionnaire as well as Hatfield and Sprecher's (1986) PLS. Contrary to our expectations, if not the authors,' reported frequency of sexual desire was not correlated with PLS scores. However, this finding is not so surprising when we consider the following circumstances. For example, the authors employed rather coarse frequency measures of sexual desire (eight response options ranging from "never" to "several times a day") that may not have captured adequately the amount of desire actually experienced by the participants. A more important criticism concerns the correlation of PLS scores with frequency of desire rather than some other more appropriate variable such as amount of desire experienced within the relationship or for the partner. The notion that sexual desire is an aspect of romantic love does not mean that an individual cannot experience desire in the absence of romantic love. That is, two individuals, one intensely in love and with a high PLS score and the other only casually dating and with a low PLS score, may experience sexual desire with the same frequency. However, it is possible that the individual who is in love experiences a desire to engage in sexual activities with the same beloved individual on 10 different occasions, whereas the other experiences sexual desire toward 10 different individuals on as many occasions. Alternately, the "in love" person may experience more intense desire toward his or her partner than someone who is not in love, although each experiences the same number of separate desire episodes. In short, we would not necessarily expect individuals with low PLS scores to experience low frequencies of sexual desire or high scorers to report frequent occurrences of sexual desire, and thus Beck et al.'s (1991) conclusions must be viewed with caution.

A series of studies conducted by Berscheid and colleagues provides a more convincing examination of the sexual desire-romantic love connection. These researchers argue that the experience of "love" is fundamentally different from the experience of being "in love," and they present evidence that romantic or passionate love (the state of being "in love") is characterized by a greater amount of sexual attraction than "love." For example, Ridge and Berscheid (1989) asked a sample of undergraduate men and women whether they believed there was a difference between the experience of being in love with and that of loving another person: Fully 87% emphatically claimed that there was a difference between the two experiences. In addition, when asked to specify the nature of that difference in an open-ended response format, participants were more likely to cite sexual attraction (i.e., sexual desire) as descriptive of the "in love" experience.

More recently, using what they term a "social categorical method," Berscheid and Meyers (1996; also see Meyers & Berscheid, 1996) asked a large sample of undergraduate men and women to list the initials of all the people they currently loved, the initials of all those with whom they were currently in love, and the initials of all those toward whom they currently felt sexual attraction/desire. For each individual respondent, the authors calculated the probability that persons named in the "sexually desire" category were also named in the "in love" and "love" categories. These sets of probabilities then were averaged across respondents. The results indicated that 85% of the persons listed in the "in love" category were also listed in the "sexually desire" category, whereas only 2% of those listed in the "love" category (and not cross-listed in the "in love" category) were listed in the

TABLE 7.1 Features of Romantic Love

Rank	Feature	Frequency
1	Trust	80.0
2	**Sexual desire**	65.8
3	Acceptance/tolerance	50.8
4	Share thoughts/secrets	44.2
5	Spend time together	44.2
6	Honesty	40.0
7	Personal sacrifice	40.0
8	Companionship/friendship	39.2
9	Jealousy	37.5
10	Communication	36.7
		...
18	**Sexual activity**	25.0
		...
25	**Touching/holding**	17.5
		...
55	**Kissing**	10.0
		...

NOTE: Frequency refers to the percentage of respondents who spontaneously cited each item in their free response definitions of the concept of romantic love. Bold items refer to sexual features.

"sexually desire" category. Thus, the objects of respondents' feelings of romantic love (but not their feelings of love) also tended to be the objects of their desire.

Research conducted by Regan and her colleagues also provides evidence that romantic love is a qualitatively different experience from other varieties of interpersonal attraction such as loving and liking and that sexual desire in particular is one of its essential components. For example, Regan, Kocan, and Whitlock (1998) conducted a prototype study to investigate how people conceptualize the state of being in love. The prototype approach (e.g., Rosch, 1975, 1978) is a standard social cognition paradigm used to investigate how people organize or represent a concept—such as romantic love—in their cognitive systems, and it allows researchers to determine the central (highly distinguishing or essential) and peripheral (less distinguishing or essential) features of a concept. These researchers asked 120 undergraduate men and women to list in a free-response format all of the features they considered to be characteristic or prototypical of the state of romantic love ("being in love"). As indicated in Table 7.1, of 119 features spontaneously generated by the participants, sexual desire received the second highest frequency rating (65.8%). In other words, when thinking of romantic love, two-thirds of the participants automatically thought of sexual desire. In addition, this feature was viewed as more important to the romantic love concept than kissing (cited by only 10% of participants), touching/holding (cited by 17.5%), and sexual activity (cited by 25%). These results certainly support the notion that sexual desire is more essential to the romantic love experience than behavioral sexual events, at least in the minds of young adults.

Two recent person perception experiments conducted by Regan (1998b) provide additional support for these prototype results. Person perception experiments are commonly used in social psychological research and essentially involve manipulating people's perceptions of a relationship and then measuring the impact of that manipulation on their subsequent evaluations and beliefs. In the first experiment, Regan provided a sample of 60 undergraduate men and women with two self-report questionnaires ostensibly completed by "Rob" and "Nancy," a student couple enrolled at the same university. The members of this couple reported experiencing no sexual desire for each other or a high amount of sexual desire for each other and were currently engaging in sexual activity with each other or were not sexually active. Participants then estimated the likelihood that the partners experience romantic love as well as a variety of other relationship events. As illustrated in Table 7.2, the results indicated that both men and women believed that dating partners who experience sexual desire for each other are more likely to be romantically in love with each other (as well as more likely to experience a variety of other relationship events) than dating partners who do not desire each other sexually, regardless of their current level of sexual activity.

A second experiment, a conceptual replication of the first, confirmed these results. Here, 48 men and women received information about the members of a heterosexual, dating "student couple" who ostensibly reported that they were currently romantically in love with each other, that they loved each other, or that they liked each other (see Table 7.3). Participants then estimated the likelihood that the

TABLE 7.2 The Impact of Sexual Desire and Sexual Activity on Perceived Likelihood of Relationship Phenomena

Sexual Desire:	Present			Absent		
Sexual Activity:	Present	Absent	Overall	Present	Absent	Overall
Romantic Love	7.53	6.47	7.00[a]	2.00	2.47	2.23[a]
Liking	8.13	8.07	8.10[a]	4.73	6.33	5.53[a]
Happiness	7.73	7.40	7.57[a]	3.60	5.60	4.60[a]
Satisfaction	7.73	7.13	7.43[a]	2.93	5.20	4.07[a]
Commitment	7.27	7.40	7.33[b]	5.60	5.33	5.47[b]
Trust	7.20	7.27	7.23[a]	5.73	6.27	6.00[a]
Loving	6.40	5.47	5.93[a]	3.07	3.80	3.43[a]

NOTES: a. Univariate follow-up analyses (applying Bonferroni protection to guard against inflating the Type I error rate and using a familywise error rate of .05) revealed that the means in this row are significantly different at $p < .001$.
b. The means in this row differ at $p < .005$.

members of the couple experience sexual desire for each other and the amount of desire that they feel for each other. Analyses revealed that participants perceived couples who are romantically in love as more *likely* to experience sexual desire than couples who love each other or who like each other. Similarly, couples who are romantically in love were believed to experience a greater *amount* of sexual desire for each other than couples who love each other or who like each other. Interestingly, sexual desire was believed to be no more likely in a "loving" relationship than in a "liking" relationship, and greater amounts of sexual desire were not believed to occur in loving relationships than liking relationships. Again, it seems that sexual desire is viewed, at least by young men and women, as an important feature or component of romantic love relationships—and not of relationships characterized by feelings of love and/or liking.

Research with actual dating couples, although sparse, also suggests that sexual desire and romantic or passionate love share a unique connection. For example, Regan (in press) found that the self-reported amount of sexual desire experienced by men and women for their dating partners was significantly positively correlated with the level of passionate love they felt for those individuals. Their feelings of desire were unrelated, however, to the amount of companionate love and liking they experienced for their partners.

TABLE 7.3 Mean Ratings of Sexual Phenomena as a Function of Couple's Relationship Status

	"Rob" and "Nancy" Report Feeling:		
	Romantic Love ("being in love")	Love	Liking
Amount of Sexual Desire	7.31[a,b]	5.94[a]	4.87[b]
Likelihood of Sexual Desire	7.81[a,b]	5.94[a]	4.81[b]
Likelihood of Sexual Intercourse	7.38[a]	5.94[b]	3.75[a,b]

NOTE: A priori comparisons using the Bonferroni procedure to control the Type I error rate and a familywise error rate of .05 revealed that means with the same superscript in each row are significantly different at $p < .01$.

✒ Conclusions

In this chapter, we considered theory and research on the nature of romantic love—in particular, its association with sexual desire. Although historically, theorists from a variety of disciplines emphasized the link between romantic love and sexual desire, for many years, social psychologists included other aspects of sexuality in their conceptualizations (or ignored sexuality entirely). However, contemporary social psychological discourse on romantic love seems to have rediscovered sexual desire, and a growing number of empirical studies now suggest that sexual desire is perceived by men and women to be an important or necessary feature of the experience of being in love.

We believe that it is important to recognize that sexual desire is not sufficient for the individual to experience romantic love toward the sexually desired other. Additional, positive but nonsexual, feelings and events must be present before most people reach the conclusion that they are "in love." However, sexual desire may spark those other, positive feelings and events (e.g., companionate love) and, similarly, companionate love for another may, given appropriate circumstances, spark sexual desire. The elements of companionate love (e.g., trust, caring, intimacy, responsivity) and sexual desire appear to be necessary to the experience of romantic love. Sexual desire can, and often does, occur in the absence of romantic love; however, it appears that the reverse is unlikely to be true in present-day American society. In sum, what we are suggesting is that sexual desire is the ingredient that

Theorist(s)/Researcher(s)	Sexual Component(s)	Necessary?	Sufficient?
1. Krafft-Ebing (1886/1945)	Sexual Desire	Yes	No
2. H. Ellis (1933/1963)	Sexual desire	Yes	No
3. Freud (1908/1963a)	Sexual desire	Yes	Yes
(1912/1963c)	Sexual desire	Yes	No
4. A. Ellis (1954)	Sexual desire	Yes	Yes
5. Reik (1944)	Sexual Desire	Yes	No
6. Fromm (1956)	Sexual desire	?	No
7. Lewis (1960)	Sexual desire	Yes	No
8. Swensen (1961)	Sexual activity	?	No
9. Rubin (1970, 1973)	None	—	—
10. Walster & Berscheid (1971) (see Hatfield)	Sexual satisfaction	?	No
11. Bardis (1971)	Sexual activity	?	?
12. Driscoll, Davis, & Lipetz (1972)	Physical attraction	Yes	No
13. Dion & Dion (1973)	None	—	—
14. Lee (1973, 1988)	Sexual attraction	Yes	No
	Sexual Activity	Yes	No
15. Pam, Plutchik, & Conte (1975)	Sexual attraction	?	No
16. Hatfield & Walster (1978)	Sexual arousal	?	No
	Sexual attraction	?	No
	Sexual excitement	?	No
Hatfield & Sprecher (1986)	Sexual desire	Yes	No
Hatfield & Rapson (1987)	Sexual desire	?	?
17. Tennov (1979)	Sexual attraction	Yes	No
18. Sternberg (1986, 1988)	Physical attraction	Yes	No
19. Hendrick & Hendrick (1986)	Physical attraction	Yes	No
	Sexual involvement	Yes	No
	Sexual satisfaction	Yes	No
20. Critelli, Myers, & Loos (1986)	Sexual arousal	Yes	No
	Physical attraction	Yes	No

Figure 7.1.

Theorist(s)/Researcher(s)	Sexual Component(s)	Necessary?	Sufficient?
21. Branden (1988)	Sexual attraction	Yes	No
22. Brehm (1988)	Sexual desire	No	No
	Sexual activity	No	No
23. Buss (1988)	Sexual activity	Yes	No
24. Murstein (1988)	Physical attraction	?	No
	Passion	?	No
25. Shaver, Hazan, & Bradshaw (1988)	Sexual system (i.e., desire, arousal, behavior, orgasm)	Yes	No
Shaver & Hazan (1988)	Sexual attraction	Yes	No
	Sexual activity	Yes	No
26. Hatfield (1988)	Sexual attraction	Yes	No
27. Berscheid (1988)	Sexual desire	Yes	No
28. Berscheid & Meyers (1996)	Sexual desire	Yes	No
29. Regan (1998a)	Sexual desire	Yes	No

Figure 7.1. *(continued)*

NOTE: Role played by sexual phenomena in theoretical and empirical conceptualizations of romantic love. Sexual desire figured prominently in early theoretical conceptualizations, and was viewed as a necessary (and, in some cases, as a sufficient) prerequisite for romantic love. Beginning in the 1960's and continuing through the mid-1980's, however, sexual desire was excluded from romantic love theory and research. Recently, sexual desire has regained a foothold in conceptualizations of romantic love.

puts the "romantic" in romantic love. A person who does not sexually desire his or her partner may like, love, care for, or even altruistically be willing to die for that individual, but he or she is not likely to be romantically or passionately in love with that person.

❧ NOTE

1. Readers should be aware that much of the early research on romantic love is predicated on the assumption that romantic love is a heterosexual experience. For example, Driscoll, Davis, and Lipetz (1972) defined romantic love as "a distinct form of interpersonal attraction that occurs between opposite-sex partners under specifiable social conditions" (p. 1), Dion and Dion (1973) discussed it as an intense form of "heterosexual attraction" (p. 55), Rubin (1970) designed his romantic love scale to assess

"love between unmarried opposite-sex peers, of the sort which could possibly lead to marriage" (p. 266), and Critelli, Myers, and Loos (1986) viewed the phenomenon as one of several "positive heterosexual attitudes and affects" (p. 356). Romantic love is most certainly not the sole province of heterosexual individuals. However, as a result of this heterosexist bias (see Herek, Kimmel, Amaro, & Melton, 1991, for an extensive discussion of this problem), many researchers interested in romantic love have limited their samples to self-labeled heterosexuals or to couples composed of opposite-sex persons. This may reduce the generalizability of their results.

8

Sexual Desire
Future Directions

W hat is sexual desire? How is it different from other sexual
responses? What causes sexual desire? What variables
influence its expression and experience? Is sexual desire related to
the feeling of being in love? If so, how? Our purpose in writing
this volume was to provide some answers to these questions by
considering the history and theories of sexual desire and by reviewing the empirical research on this fascinating life experience.
In the process of conducting our investigations and writing our
conclusions, however, we realized that there remains much to be
learned about sexual desire.

☙ Future Research Directions

For example, the majority of research on sexual desire has focused
on the nature of sexual desire and its causal antecedents. We believe

that it is equally, if not more, important to understand and investigate the individual and interpersonal *consequences* of sexual desire. For example, the fact that most of us seem to link sexual desire and romantic love may have implications for understanding the dynamics of sexual interactions. It is possible, for instance, that a man may express feelings of love, intimacy, and commitment in an attempt to excite his partner's feelings of sexual desire and increase the likelihood of sexual activity. Moreover, assuming that sexual desire in women is inevitably triggered by declarations of love and commitment, he may view these "romantic" events as adequate justification for the occurrence of forcible sexual activity. Conversely, a woman who believes that she ought to experience desire after receiving an expression of intimacy or love from a dating partner may be uncertain as to how to interpret, and consequently less likely to report, a sexually violent encounter.

Some research suggests, in fact, that romantic events or expressions that occur during a sexual interaction may alter perceptions of that interaction. Regan (1997) asked men and women to read one of two versions of a scenario involving an interaction between a heterosexual, dating couple. In each scenario, the couple has rented a movie and returned to the man's room to view the video; during the movie, "Bob" expresses to "Cathy" his interest in sexual activity. Half of the participants read a scenario in which Bob confesses his feelings of romantic love for Cathy prior to requesting sex; the other half simply read his sexual request. Both scenarios continue with Bob initiating sexual activity, Cathy verbally refusing, and the date ending in sexual intercourse. The results revealed that when Bob expressed his feelings of romantic love for Cathy, he was perceived as less likely to have sexually assaulted her. Conversely, when Cathy received a verbal declaration of love from Bob, she was viewed as more likely to have experienced sexual desire and to have wanted sexual intercourse—despite her clearly stated unwillingness—than when she received an expression of sexual interest. Finally, the sexual interaction was perceived as significantly more consensual (i.e., reflecting the mutual desires of the partners) when Bob professed love than when he professed sexual intent. More important, however, Cathy's perceived sexual desire level mediated the effect of Bob's sexual request style (romantic vs. sexual) on the perceived likelihood of consensual sex. In plain

English, the expression of romantic love by Bob significantly increased the likelihood that his subsequent sexual interaction with the unwilling Cathy was labeled "consensual" *because perceivers assumed that this expression of love caused Cathy to feel sexual desire and to want sex.* The fact that we in this culture have so firmly linked romantic love with sexual desire may contribute to sexual dynamics, communication, and miscommunication; may influence the labels we place on sexual interactions; and may even result in sexually inappropriate behavior. We hope that future researchers will continue to explore not only the consequences of beliefs about desire and love but the ways in which men and women allow their behaviors to be guided by these beliefs and expectations in their actual, ongoing interactions.

And this brings us to another point. Because sexual desire is often experienced and expressed within close relationships, it is related to many other relationship phenomena. Indeed, Chapter 7 was devoted in its entirety to an exploration of the link between sexual desire and one of the most important of these relationship phenomena—namely, romantic love. Unfortunately, there has been relatively little research that considers both the experience and the expression of sexual desire from within a relational context. The majority of the research on the causal antecedents of sexual desire (e.g., hormones, age, mood, drugs) has focused on the individual experience of desire—amount and frequency. Most researchers do not appear to recognize that there may be a significant difference between a person's feelings of sexual desire in general and his or her feelings of sexual desire for the relationship partner. In addition, most have not asked their participants about other, interpersonal factors that may significantly influence self-reports of sexual desire.

Similarly, other than clinical anecdotes about couples with sexual desire problems, we know very little about the role that sexual desire plays within ongoing, interpersonal relationships (particularly healthy, functioning relationships). Certainly men and women *believe* that the presence or absence of sexual desire within a relationship has implications for the emotional tenor and interpersonal dynamics of that relationship. Regan's (1998b) study, reviewed in the last chapter, demonstrated that people view partners who desire each other sexually as more likely to experience not only romantic love but also a host of other positive interpersonal phenomena, including happiness, liking, commitment, and trust. Similarly, in couples whose relationship was characterized by a discrepancy in sexual desire (i.e., one person experienced high sexual desire for a nonreciprocating partner), the sexually interested partner was perceived as significantly more likely than the sexually uninterested partner to be satisfied and happy with the partner; the partner with low sexual desire, however, was viewed as significantly more likely to terminate the relationship and to be unfaithful. At least when evaluating other couples, people appear to use sexual desire to gauge relationship quality and adjustment. It remains for future research to investigate whether the waxing and waning of sexual desire within a relationship actually correspond to the ebb and flow of other interpersonally significant events.

ᴥ Concluding Remarks

We end this volume by simply noting that sexual desire has profound implications for the quality of human life. We have reviewed a large body of empirical evidence that suggests that as a person's physical, emotional, and psychological state fluctuates, so too does his or her ability and motivation to experience and express sexual desire. In addition, we have discussed the ways in which sexual desire may contribute to, or even cause a person to feel, romantic love. Understanding sexual desire—what it is, how it differs from other aspects of sexuality, what mental and physical factors influence its expression, how it is related to interpersonal phenomena such as romantic love—is one very important step in learning how to communicate about sexual desire. And learning how to communicate one's feelings of sexual desire (or lack thereof) to a sexual and/or romantic partner is critical to personal well-being and interpersonal satisfaction. Can we live without sexual desire? Most definitely. Would we want to live without it? Probably not.

References

Abbey, A. (1982). Sex differences in attributions for friendly behavior: Do males misperceive females' friendliness? *Journal of Personality and Social Psychology, 42,* 830-838.

Abbey, A. (1987). Misperceptions of friendly behavior as sexual interest: A survey of naturally occurring incidents. *Psychology of Women Quarterly, 11,* 173-194.

Abbey, A., & Melby, C. (1986). The effects of nonverbal cues on gender differences in perceptions of sexual intent. *Sex Roles, 15,* 283-298.

Abel, E. L. (1985). *Psychoactive drugs and sex.* New York: Plenum.

Abplanalp, J. M., Rose, R. M., Donnelly, A. F., & Livingstone-Vaughan, L. (1979). Psychoendocrinology of the menstrual cycle: II. The relationship between enjoyment of activities, moods and reproductive hormones. *Psychosomatic Medicine, 41,* 605-615.

Adams, A. E., III, Haynes, S. N., & Brayer, M. A. (1985). Cognitive distraction in female sexual arousal. *Psychophysiology, 22,* 689-696.

Adams, D. B., Gold, A. R., & Burt, A. D. (1978). Rise in female-initiated sexual activity at ovulation and its suppression by oral contraceptives. *New England Journal of Medicine, 299,* 1145-1150.

Alder, E. M., Cook, A., Davidson, D., West, C., & Bancroft, J. (1986). Hormones, mood and sexuality in lactating women. *British Journal of Psychiatry, 148,* 74-79.

Alexander, G. M., Sherwin, B. B., Bancroft, J., & Davidson, D. W. (1990). Testosterone and sexual behavior in oral contraceptive users and nonusers: A prospective study. *Hormones and Behavior, 24,* 388-402.

Allen, J. B., Kenrick, D. T., Linder, D. E., & McCall, M. A. (1989). Arousal and attraction: A response-facilitation alternative to misattribution and negative-reinforcement models. *Journal of Personality and Social Psychology, 57,* 261-270.

Antonovsky, H., Sadowsky, M., & Maoz, B. (1990). Sexual activity of aging men and women: An Israeli study. *Behavior, Health, and Aging, 1,* 151-161.

Appelt, H., & Strauss, B. (1986). The psychoendocrinology of female sexuality: A research project. *German Journal of Psychology, 10,* 143-1256.

Argyle, M., & Dean, J. (1965). Eye-contact, distance, and affiliation. *Sociometry, 28,* 289-304.

Arnett, J. L., Prosen, H., & Toews, J. A. (1986). Loss of libido due to stress. *Medical Aspects of Human Sexuality, 20,* 140-148.

Azar, B. (1998, January). Communicating through pheromones. *APA Monitor, 29,* 1, 12.

Baird, D. T. (1976). Oestrogens in clinical practice. In J. A. Loraine & E. T. Bell (Eds.), *Hormone assays and their clinical application* (4th ed., pp. 408-446). Edinburgh: Churchill Livingstone.

Bakke, J. L. (1965). A double-blind study of a progestin-estrogen combination in the management of the menopause. *Pacific Medicine & Surgery, 73,* 200-205.

Bancroft, J. (1984). Hormones and human sexual behavior. *Journal of Sex & Marital Therapy, 10,* 3-21.

Bancroft, J. (1988). Sexual desire and the brain. *Sexual and Marital Therapy, 3,* 11-27.

Bancroft, J., O'Carroll, R., McNeilly, A., & Shaw, R. W. (1984). The effects of bromocriptine on the sexual behavior of a hyperprolactinaemic man: A controlled case study. *Clinical Endocrinology, 21,* 131-137.

Bancroft, J., Sanders, D., Davidson, D., & Warner, P. (1983). Mood, sexuality, hormones, and the menstrual cycle. III. Sexuality and the role of androgens. *Psychosomatic Medicine, 45,* 509-516.

Bancroft, J., Tennent, G., Loucas, K., & Cass, J. (1974). The control of deviant sexual behaviour by drugs: I. Behavioural changes following oestrogens and anti-androgens. *British Journal of Psychiatry, 125,* 310-315.

Bardis, P. D. (1971). Erotometer: A technique for the measurement of heterosexual love. *International Review of Sociology, 1,* 71-77.

Barling, J., & Fincham, F. (1980). Alcohol, psychological conservatism, and sexual interest in male social drinkers. *Journal of Social Psychology, 112,* 135-144.

Beach, F. A. (1976). Sexual attractivity, proceptivity, and receptivity in female mammals. *Hormones and Behavior, 7,* 105-138.

Beck, A. T. (1967). *Depression: Clinical, experimental and theoretical aspects.* London: Staples.

Beck, J. G., Bozman, A. W., & Qualtrough, T. (1991). The experience of sexual desire: Psychological correlates in a college sample. *Journal of Sex Research, 28,* 443-456.

Beck, S., Ward-Hull, C., & McLear, P. (1976). Variables related to women's somatic preferences of the male and female body. *Journal of Personality and Social Psychology, 34,* 1200-1210.

Beigel, H. G. (1951). Romantic love. *American Sociological Review, 16,* 326-334.

Bell, D. S., & Trethowan, W. H. (1961). Amphetamine addiction and disturbed sexuality. *Archives of General Psychiatry, 4,* 100-104.

Benedek, T., & Rubenstein, B. B. (1939a). The correlations between ovarian activity and psychodynamic processes: I. The ovulative phase. *Psychosomatic Medicine, 1,* 245-270.

Benedek, T., & Rubenstein, B. B. (1939b). The correlations between ovarian activity and psychodynamic processes: II. The menstrual phase. *Psychosomatic Medicine, 1,* 461-485.

Benedek, T. B. (1977). Ambivalence, passion, and love. *Journal of the American Psychoanalytic Association, 25,* 53-79.

Benjamin, F., & Seltzer, V. L. (1987). The menopause and perimenopause. In Z. Rosenwaks, F. Benjamin, & M. L. Stone (Eds.), *Gynecology: Principles and practice* (pp. 165-187). New York: Macmillan.

Benton, D. (1982). The influence of androstenol—a putative human pheromone—on mood throughout the menstrual cycle. *Biological Psychology, 15,* 249-256.

Benton, D., & Wastell, V. (1986). Effects of androstenol on human sexual arousal. *Biological Psychology, 22,* 141-147.

Berlin, F. S., & Meinecke, C. F. (1981). Treatment of sex offenders with antiandrogenic medication: Conceptualization, review of treatment modalities, and preliminary findings. *American Journal of Psychiatry, 138,* 601-607.

Berliner, D. L., Jennings-White, C., & Lavker, R. M. (1991). The human skin: Fragrances and pheromones. *Journal of Steroid Biochemistry and Molecular Biology, 39,* 671-679.

Bermant, G. (1976). Sexual behavior: Hard times with the Coolidge effect. In M. H. Siegel & H. P. Zeigler (Eds.), *Psychological research: The inside story* (pp. 76-103). New York: Harper & Row.

Berry, M. S., & Brain, P. F. (1986). Neurophysiological and endocrinological consequences of alcohol. In P. F. Brain (Ed.), *Alcohol and aggression* (pp. 19-54). Dover, NH: Croom Helm.

Berscheid, E. (1985). Interpersonal attraction. In G. Lindzey & E. Aronson (Eds.), *The handbook of social psychology* (3rd ed., Vol. 2, pp. 413-484). New York: Random House.

Berscheid, E. (1988). Some comments on love's anatomy: Or, whatever happened to old-fashioned lust? In R. J. Sternberg & M. L. Barnes (Eds.), *The psychology of love* (pp. 359-374). New Haven, CT: Yale University Press.

Berscheid, E., & Meyers, S. A. (1996). A social categorical approach to a question about love. *Personal Relationships, 3,* 19-43.

Berscheid, E., & Walster, E. (1974a). A little bit about love. In T. L. Huston (Ed.), *Foundations of interpersonal attraction* (pp. 355-381). New York: Academic Press.

Berscheid, E., & Walster, E. (1974b). Physical attractiveness. In L. Berkowitz (Ed.), *Advances in experimental social psychology* (Vol. 7, pp. 157-215). New York: Academic Press.

Bertocci, P. A. (1988). *The person and primary emotions.* New York: Springer-Verlag.

Beumont, P. J. V., Abraham, S. F., & Simson, K. G. (1981). The psychosexual histories of adolescent girls and young women with anorexia nervosa. *Psychological Medicine, 11,* 131-140.

Black, S. L., & Biron, C. (1982). Androstenol as a human pheromone: No effect on perceived physical attractiveness. *Behavioral and Neural Biology, 34,* 326-330.

Bohlen, J. G., Held, J. P., & Sanderson, M. O. (1983). Update on sexual physiology research. In J. W. Maddock, G. Neubeck, & M. B. Sussman (Eds.), *Human sexuality and the family* (pp. 21-33). New York: Haworth.

Bozman, A. W., & Beck, J. G. (1991). Covariation of sexual desire and sexual arousal: The effects of anger and anxiety. *Archives of Sexual Behavior, 20,* 47-60.

Branden, N. (1988). A vision of romantic love. In R. J. Sternberg & M. L. Barnes (Eds.), *The psychology of love* (pp. 218-231). New Haven, CT: Yale University Press.

Brehm, S. S. (1988). Passionate love. In R. J. Sternberg & M. L. Barnes (Eds.), *The psychology of love* (pp. 232-263). New Haven, CT: Yale University Press.

Briere, J. (1984, April). *The effects of childhood sexual abuse on later psychological functioning: Defining a "post-sexual-abuse syndrome."* Paper presented at the Third National Conference on Sexual Victimization of Children, Washington, DC.

Brincat, M., Studd, J. W. W., O'Dowd, T., Magos, A., Cardozo, L. D., Wardle, P. J., & Cooper, D. (1984, January). Subcutaneous hormone implants for the control of climacteric symptoms: A prospective study. *The Lancet,* pp. 16-18.

Brooks, R. V. (1984). Androgens: Physiology and pathology. In H. L. J. Makin (Ed.), *Biochemistry of steroid hormones* (2nd ed., pp. 565-594). Oxford, UK: Blackwell Scientific Publications.

Brooksbank, B. W. L., Brown, R., & Gustafsson, J. A. (1974). The detection of 5-alpha-androst-16-en-3-alpha-ol in human male axillary sweat. *Experientia, 30,* 864-865.

Brown, W. A., Monti, P. M., & Corriveau, D. P. (1978). Serum testosterone and sexual activity and interest in men. *Archives of Sexual Behavior, 7,* 97-103.

Browne, A., & Finkelhor, D. (1986). Impact of child sexual abuse: A review of the research. *Psychological Bulletin, 99,* 66-77.

Buckman, M. T., & Kellner, R. (1985). Reduction of distress in hyperprolactinemia with bromocriptine. *American Journal of Psychiatry, 142,* 242-244.

Buffum, J. (1982). Pharmacosexology: The effects of drugs on sexual function. *Journal of Psychoactive Drugs, 14,* 5-44.

Buffum, J., Moser, C., & Smith, D. (1988). Street drugs and sexual function. In J. M. A. Sitsen (Ed.), *Handbook of sexology: Vol. VI. The pharmacology and endocrinology of sexual function* (pp. 462-477). Amsterdam: Elsevier Science Publishers.

Burger, H. G., Hailes, J., Menelaus, M., Nelson, J., Hudson, B., & Balazs, N. (1984). The management of persistent menopausal symptoms with oestradiol-testosterone implants: Clinical, lipid and hormonal results. *Maturitas, 6,* 351-358.

Burgess, E. W., & Wallin, P. (1953). *Engagement and marriage.* Philadelphia, PA: J. B. Lippincott.

Burt, M. R. (1980). Cultural myths and supports for rape. *Journal of Personality and Social Psychology, 38,* 217-230.

Buss, D. M. (1988). Love acts: The evolutionary biology of love. In R. J. Sternberg & M. L. Barnes (Eds.), *The psychology of love* (pp. 100-118). New Haven, CT: Yale University Press.

Buss, D. M., & Kenrick, D. T. (1998). Evolutionary social psychology. In D. T. Gilbert, S. T. Fiske, & G. Lindzey (Eds.), *The handbook of social psychology* (4th ed., Vol. 2, pp. 982-1026). New York: McGraw-Hill.

Buss, D. M., & Schmitt, D. P. (1993). Sexual strategies theory: An evolutionary perspective on human mating. *Psychological Review, 100,* 204-232.

Butler, R. N., & Lewis, M. I. (1976). *Love and sex after sixty.* New York: Harper & Row.

Butler, R. N., & Lewis, M. I. (1986). *Love and sex after 40.* New York: Harper & Row.

Buunk, B. (1984). Jealousy as related to attributions for the partners' behavior. *Social Psychology Quarterly, 47,* 107-112.

Byers, E. S., & Heinlein, L. (1989). Predicting initiations and refusals of sexual activities in married and cohabiting heterosexual couples. *Journal of Sex Research, 26,* 210-231.

Byrne, D. (1977). Social psychology and the study of sexual behavior. *Personality and Social Psychology Bulletin, 3,* 3-30.

Byrne, D. (1983a). The antecedents, correlates, and consequents or erotophobia-erotophilia. In C. Davis (Ed.), *Challenges in sexual science: Current theoretical issues and research advances* (pp. 53-75). Philadelphia, PA: Society for the Scientific Study of Sex.

Byrne, D. (1983b). Sex without contraception. In D. Byrne & W. A. Fisher (Eds.), *Adolescents, sex, and contraception* (pp. 3-31). Hillsdale, NJ: Lawrence Erlbaum.

Campbell, S. (1976). Double-blind psychometric studies on the effects of natural estrogens on post-menopausal women. In S. Campbell (Ed.), *The management of the menopausal and post-menopausal years* (pp.149-158). Baltimore, MD: University Park Press.

Campbell, S., & Whitehead, M. (1977). Oestrogen therapy and the menopausal syndrome. *Clinical Obstetrics and Gynecology, 4,* 31-47.

Cardozo, L., Gibb, D. M. F., Tuck, S. M., Thom, M. H., Studd, J. W. W., & Cooper, D. J. (1984). The effects of subcutaneous hormone implants during the climacteric. *Maturitas, 5,* 177-184.

Carney, A., Bancroft, J., & Mathews, A. (1978). Combination of hormonal and psychological treatment for female sexual unresponsiveness: A comparative study. *British Journal of Psychiatry, 133,* 339-346.

Carter, J. N., Tyson, J. E., Tolis, G., Van Vliet, S., Faiman, C., & Friesen, H. G. (1978). Prolactin-secreting tumors and hypogonadism in 22 men. *New England Journal of Medicine, 299,* 847-852.

Cash, T. F., Gillen, B., & Burns, D. S. (1977). Sexism and "beautyism" in personnel consultant decision making. *Journal of Applied Psychology, 62,* 301-310.

Cash, T. F., Rissi, J., & Chapman, R. (1985). Not just another pretty face: Sex roles, locus of control, and cosmetics use. *Personality and Social Psychology Bulletin, 11*(3), 246-257.

Casper, R. C., Redmond, E., Katz, M. M., Schaffer, C. B., Davis, J. M., & Koslow, S. H. (1985). Somatic symptoms in primary affective disorder. *Archives of General Psychiatry, 42,* 1098-1104.

Cavanagh, J. R. (1969). Rhythm of sexual desire in women. *Medical Aspects of Human Sexuality, 3,* 29-39.

Cernoch, J. M., & Porter, R. H. (1985). Recognition of maternal axillary odors in infants. *Child Development, 56,* 1593-1598.

Channon, L. D., & Ballinger, S. E. (1986). Some aspects of sexuality and vaginal symptoms during menopause and their relation to anxiety and depression. *British Journal of Medical Psychology, 59,* 173-180.

Chaturvedi, S. K., & Chandra, P. S. (1990). Stress-protective functions of positive experiences during the premenstrual period. *Stress Medicine, 6,* 53-55.

Christopher, F. S., Owens, L. A., & Stecker, H. L. (1993). Exploring the darkside of courtship: A test of a model of male premarital sexual aggressiveness. *Journal of Marriage and the Family, 55,* 469-479.

Cittadini, E., & Barreca, P. (1977). Use of antiandrogens in gynecology. In L. Martini & M. Motta (Eds.), *International symposium on androgens and antiandrogens, Milan, 1976* (pp. 309-319). New York: Raven.

Clark, A. J. (1952). *Applied pharmacology* (8th ed.). Philadelphia: Blakiston.

Clayson, D. E., & Klassen, M. L. (1989). Perception of attractiveness by obesity and hair color. *Perceptual and Motor Skills, 68,* 199-202.

Cohn, B. A. (1994). In search of human skin pheromones. *Archives of Dermatology, 130*, 1048-1051.

Connell, C. (1965). *Aphrodisiacs in your garden*. London: Arthur Barker.

Connell, P. H. (1958). *Amphetamine psychosis*. London: Chapman & Hall.

Coope, J. (1976). Double-blind cross-over study of estrogen replacement. In S. Campbell (Ed.), *The management of the menopausal and post-menopausal years* (pp. 159-168). Baltimore, MD: University Park Press.

Cooper, A. J. (1986). Progestogens in the treatment of male sex offenders: A review. *Canadian Journal of Psychiatry, 31*, 73-79.

Cooper, A. J., Ismail, A. A. A., Phanjoo, A. L., & Love, D. L. (1972). Antiandrogen (cyproterone acetate) therapy in deviant hypersexuality. *British Journal of Psychiatry, 120*, 59-63.

Craine, L. S., Henson, C. E., Colliver, J. A., & MacLean, D. G. (1988). Prevalence of a history of sexual abuse among female psychiatric patients in a state hospital system. *Hospital and Community Psychiatry, 39*, 300-304.

Cremoncini, C., Vignati, E., & Libroia, A. (1977). Treatment of hirsutism and acne in women with 2 combinations of CPA and EE. *Acta Europaea Fertilitatis, 7*, 299-314.

Crenshaw, T. L., & Goldberg, J. P. (1996). *Sexual pharmacology: Drugs that affect sexual functioning*. New York: Norton.

Critelli, J. W., Myers, E. J., & Loos, V. E. (1986). The components of love: Romantic attraction and sex role orientation. *Journal of Personality, 54*, 354-370.

Cunningham, M. R., Barbee, A. P., Graves, C. R., Lundy, D. E., & Lister, S. C. (1996, August). *Can't buy me love: The effects of male wealth and personal qualities on female attraction*. Paper presented at the annual convention of the American Psychological Association, Toronto, Canada.

Cunningham, M. R., Druen, P. B., & Barbee, A. P. (1997). Angels, mentors, and friends: Trade-offs among evolutionary, social, and individual variables in physical appearance. In J. A. Simpson & D. T. Kenrick (Eds.), *Evolutionary social psychology* (pp. 109-140). Mahwah, NJ: Lawrence Erlbaum.

Cushman, P. (1972). Sexual behavior in heroin addiction and methadone maintenance. *New York State Journal of Medicine, 72*, 1261-1265.

Cutler, W. B., Garcia, C. R., & McCoy, N. (1987). Perimenopausal sexuality. *Archives of Sexual Behavior, 16*, 225-234.

Cutler, W. B., Preti, G., Huggins, G. R., Erickson, B., & Garcia, C. R. (1985). Sexual behavior frequency and biphasic ovulatory type menstrual cycles. *Physiology and Behavior, 34*, 805-810.

Cutler, W. B., Preti, G., Krieger, A., Huggins, G. R., Garcia, C. R., & Lawley, H. J. (1986). Human axillary secretions influence women's menstrual cycles: The role of donor extract from men. *Hormones and Behavior, 20*, 463-473.

Darwin, C. (1859). *On the origin of the species by means of natural selection, or, preservation of favoured races in the struggle for life*. London: J. Murray.

Darwin, C. (1871). *The descent of man, and selection in relation to sex.* London: J. Murray.

Dashiell, J. F. (1928). *Fundamentals of objective psychology.* Boston, MA: Houghton Mifflin.

Davidson, J. K., Sr. (1985). The utilization of sexual fantasies by sexually experienced university students. *Journal of American College Health, 34,* 24-32.

Davidson, J. M., Camargo, C. A., & Smith, E. R. (1979). Effects of androgen on sexual behavior in hypogonadal men. *Journal of Clinical Endocrinology & Metabolism, 48,* 955-958.

Davis, K. B. (1926). Periodicity of sex desire. Part I. Unmarried women, college graduates. *American Journal of Obstetrics and Gynecology, 12,* 824-838.

Davis-Pyles, B., Conger, J. C., & Conger, A. J. (1990). The impact of deviant weight on social competence ratings. *Behavioral Assessment, 12,* 443-455.

Dekker, J., & Everaerd, W. (1989). Psychological determinants of sexual arousal: A review. *Behaviour Research and Therapy, 27,* 353-364.

Dekker, J., Everaerd, W., & Verhelst, N. (1985). Attending to stimuli or to images of sexual feelings: Effects on sexual arousal. *Behaviour Research and Therapy, 23,* 139-149.

DeLamater, J. (1987). Gender differences in sexual scenarios. In K. Kelley (Ed.), *Females, males, and sexuality: Theories and research* (pp. 127-139). Albany: State Uuniversity of New York Press.

DeLamater, J. (1991). Emotions and sexuality. In K. McKinney & S. Sprecher (Eds.), *Sexuality in close relationships* (pp. 49-70). Hillsdale, NJ: Lawrence Erlbaum.

De Leon, G., & Wexler, H. K. (1973). Heroin addiction: Its relation to sexual behavior and sexual experience. *Journal of Abnormal Psychology, 81,* 36-38.

Deneau, G. A., & Mule, S. J. (1981). Pharmacology of the opiates. In J. H. Lowinson & P. Ruiz (Eds.), *Substance abuse: Clinical problems and perspectives* (pp. 129-139). Baltimore, MD: Williams & Wilkins.

Dennerstein, L., & Burrows, G. D. (1982). Hormone replacement therapy and sexuality in women. *Clinics in Endocrinology and Metabolism, 11,* 661-679.

Dennerstein, L., Burrows, G. D., Wood, C., & Hyman, G. (1980). Hormones and sexuality: The effect of estrogen and progestogen. *Obstetrics and Gynecology, 56,* 316-322.

de Silva, P. (1993). Sexual problems in women with eating disorders. In J. M. Ussher & C. D. Baker (Eds.), *Psychological perspectives on sexual problems: New directions in theory and practice* (pp. 79-109). New York: Routledge.

Dewsbury, D. A. (1981). Effects of novelty on copulatory behavior: The Coolidge effect and related phenomena. *Psychological Bulletin, 89,* 464-482.

Dion, K., Berscheid, E., & Walster, E. (1972). What is beautiful is good. *Journal of Personality and Social Psychology, 24,* 285-290.

Dion, K. L., & Dion, K. K. (1973). Correlates of romantic love. *Journal of Consulting and Clinical Psychology, 1,* 51-56.

Douglas, N. (1931). *Paneros: Some words on aphrodisiacs and the like.* London: Chatto & Windus.

Dow, M. G. T., & Gallagher, J. (1989). A controlled study of combined hormonal and psychological treatment for sexual unresponsiveness in women. *British Journal of Clinical Psychology, 28,* 201-212.

Drago, F. (1984). Prolactin and sexual behavior: A review. *Neuroscience & Biobehavioral Reviews, 8,* 433-439.

Driscoll, R., Davis, K. E., & Lipetz, M. E. (1972). Parental interference and romantic love: The Romeo and Juliet effect. *Journal of Personality and Social Psychology, 24,* 1-10.

Dutton, D. G., & Aron, A. P. (1974). Some evidence for heightened sexual attraction under conditions of high anxiety. *Journal of Personality and Social Psychology, 30,* 510-517.

Eagly, A. H. (1987). *Sex differences in social behavior: A social-role interpretation.* Hillsdale, NJ: Lawrence Erlbaum.

Eagly, A. H., & Karau, S. J. (1991). Gender and the emergence of leaders: A meta-analysis. *Journal of Personality and Social Psychology, 60,* 685-710.

Edwards, R. (1971). The use of drugs in the search for a human aphrodisiac experience. *Journal of Drug Education, 1,* 137-145.

Eiser, J. R., & Ford, N. (1995). Sexual relationships on holiday: A case of situational disinhibition. *Journal of Social and Personal Relationships, 12,* 323-339.

Ellinwood, E. H., & Rockwell, W. J. K. (1975). Effect of drug use on sexual behavior. *Medical Aspects of Human Sexuality, 9,* 10, 14, 17-18, 23.

Ellis, A. (1954). *The American sexual tragedy.* New York, NY: Twayne.

Ellis, H. (1901-1928). *Studies in the psychology of sex* (Vols. 1-7). Philadelphia, PA: F. A. Davis. (Original work published 1897-1928)

Ellis, H. (1963). *Psychology of sex.* New York: New American Library of World Literature. (Original work published 1933)

Eskin, B. A., Aspinall, A. R., & Segrave-Daly, S. L. (1985). Effects of hormone-secreting tumors on libido. *Medical Aspects of Human Sexuality, 19,* 50-66.

Evans, P. (1989). *Motivation and emotion.* London: Routledge.

Everaerd, W. (1988). Commentary on sex research: Sex as an emotion. *Journal of Psychology and Human Sexuality, 1,* 3-15.

Faglia, G., Beck-Peccoz, P., Travaglini, P., Ambioso, B., Rondena, M., Paracchi, A., Spada, A., Welser, G., & Bouzin, A. (1977). Functional studies in hyperprolactinaemic states. In P. G. Crosignani & C. Robyn (Eds.), *Prolactin and human reproduction* (pp. 225-238). London: Academic Press.

Falicov, C. J. (1973). Sexual adjustment during first pregnancy and post partum. *American Journal of Obstetrics and Gynecology, 117,* 991-1000.

Fava, G. A., Fava, M., Kellner, R., Serafini, E., & Mastrogiacomo, I. (1981). Depression, hostility and anxiety in hyperprolactinemic amenorrhea. *Psychotherapy and Psychosomatics, 36,* 122-128.

Feingold, A. (1992). Good-looking people are not what we think. *Psychological Bulletin, 111,* 304-341.

Ferrero, G., & La Pietra, O. (1971). Libido fluctuations during the menstrual cycle. *Panminerva Medica, 13,* 407-409.

Field, L. H., & Williams, M. (1970). The hormonal treatment of sexual offenders. *Medicine, Science and the Law, 10,* 27-34.

Filler, W., & Drezner, N. (1944). The results of surgical castration in women under forty. *American Journal of Obstetrics and Gynecology, 47,* 122-124.

Filsinger, E. E., Braun, J. J., Monte, W. C., & Linder, D. E. (1984). Human (*Homo sapiens*) responses to the pig (*Sus scrofa*) sex pheromone 5 alpha-androst-16-en-3-one. *Journal of Comparative Psychology, 98,* 219-222.

Fish, L. S., Fish, R. C., & Sprenkle, D. H. (1984). Treating inhibited sexual desire: A marital therapy approach. *American Journal of Family Therapy, 12,* 3-12.

Fisher, H. (1992). *Anatomy of love: A natural history of mating, marriage, and why we stray.* New York: Fawcett Columbine.

Fisher, R. A. (1958). *The genetical theory of natural selection* (2nd ed.). Oxford, UK: Clarendon.

Fisher, W. A., Byrne, D., White, L. A., & Kelley, K. (1988). Erotophobia-erotophilia as a dimension of personality. *Journal of Sex Research , 25,* 123-151.

Fisher, W. A., & Gray, J. (1988). Erotophobia-erotophilia and sexual behavior during pregnancy and postpartum. *Journal of Sex Research , 25,* 379-396.

Ford, C. S., & Beach, F. (1951). *Patterns of sexual behavior.* New York: Harper.

Fotherby, K. (1984). Biosynthesis of the oestrogens. In H. L. J. Makin (Ed.), *Biochemistry of steroid hormones* (2nd ed., pp. 207-229). Oxford, UK: Blackwell Scientific Publications.

Franks, S., Jacobs, H. S., Martin, N., & Nabarro, J. D. N. (1978). Hyperprolactinaemia and impotence. *Clinical Endocrinology, 8,* 277-287.

Franzoi, S. L., & Herzog, M. E. (1987). Judging physical attractiveness: What body aspects do we use? *Personality and Social Psychology Bulletin, 13,* 19-33.

Freud, S. (1938). Three contributions to the theory of sex. In A. A. Brill (Ed. and Trans.), *The basic writings of Sigmund Freud* (pp. 553-629). New York: Random House. (Original work published 1905)

Freud, S. (1963a). "Civilized" sexual morality and modern nervousness. In P. Rieff (Ed.), *Sexuality and the psychology of love* (pp. 20-40). New York: Collier. (Original work published 1908)

Freud, S. (1963b). *The cocaine papers.* Vienna: Duquin. (Original work published 1884)

Freud, S. (1963c). The most prevalent form of degradation in erotic life. In P. Rieff (Ed.), *Sexuality and the psychology of love* (pp. 58-70). New York: Collier. (Original work published 1912)

Freud, S. (1977). *Five lectures on psycho-analysis* (J. Strachey, Ed. and Trans.). New York: Norton. (Original work published 1910)

Friesen, H. G., Tolis, G., Shiu, R., & Hwang, R. (1973). Studies on human prolactin: Chemistry, radio receptor assay and clinical significance. In J. L.

Pasteels & C. Robyn (Eds.), *Human prolactin* (pp. 11-23). Amsterdam: Exerpta Medica.

Fromm, E. (1956). *The art of loving*. New York: Harper & Row.

Furnham, A. F., & Radley, S. (1989). Sex differences in the perception of male and female body shapes. *Personality and Individual Differences, 10*, 653-662.

Furuhjelm, M., Karlgren, E., & Carlstrom, K. (1984). The effect of estrogen therapy on somatic and psychical symptoms in postmenopausal women. *Acta Obstetricia et Gynecologica Scandinavica, 63*, 655-661.

Gagnon, J. H. (1974). Scripts and the coordination of sexual conduct. In J. K. Cole & R. Deinstbier (Eds.), *The Nebraska symposium on motivation, 1973* (pp. 27-59). Lincoln: University of Nebraska Press.

Gagnon, J. H., & Simon, W. (1973). *Sexual conduct: The social sources of human sexuality*. Chicago: Aldine.

Gangestad, S. W. (1993). Sexual selection and physical attractiveness: Implications for mating dynamics. *Human Nature, 4*, 205-235.

Gangestad, S. W., & Simpson, J. A. (1990). Toward an evolutionary history of female sociosexual variation. *Journal of Personality, 58*, 69-96.

Garcia, L. T., Brennan, K., DeCarlo, M., McGlennon, R., & Tait, S. (1984). Sex differences in sexual arousal to different erotic stories. *Journal of Sex Research , 20*, 391-402.

Garcia-Velasco, J., & Mondragon, M. (1991). The incidence of the vomeronasal organ in 1,000 human subjects and its possible clinical significance. *Journal of Steroid Biochemistry and Molecular Biology, 39*, 561-563.

Gay, G. R., Newmeyer, J. A., Elion, R. A., & Wieder, S. (1975). Drug-sex practice in the Haight-Ashbury or "the sensuous hippie." In M. Sandler & G. L. Gessa (Eds.), *Sexual behavior: Pharmacology and biochemistry* (pp. 63-79). New York: Raven.

Gay, G. R., Newmeyer, J. A., Perry, M., Johnson, G., & Kurland, M. (1982). Love and Haight: The sensuous hippie revisited. Drug/sex practices in San Francisco, 1980-81. *Journal of Psychoactive Drugs, 14*, 111-123.

Gay, G. R., & Sheppard, C. W. (1972). Sex in the "drug culture." *Medical Aspects of Human Sexuality, 6*, 28, 30-31, 34, 37, 43-44, 47, 49-50.

Gerald, M. C., & Schwirian, P. M. (1973). Nonmedical use of methaqualone. *Archives of General Psychiatry, 28*, 627-631.

Gilmore, D. C., Beehr, T. A., & Love, K. G. (1986). Effects of applicant sex, applicant physical attractiveness, type of rater and type of job on interview decisions. *Journal of Occupational Psychology, 59*, 103-109.

Gitter, A. G., Lomranz, J., Saxe, L., & Bar-Tal, Y. (1983). Perceptions of female physique characteristics by American and Israeli students. *Journal of Social Psychology, 121*, 7-13.

Glickman, S. P., Rosenfield, R. L., Bergenstal, R. M., & Helke, J. (1982). Multiple androgenic abnormalities, including elevated free testosterone, in hyperprolactinemic women. *Journal of Clinical Endocrinology & Metabolism, 55*, 251-257.

Goldman, W., & Lewis, P. (1977). Beautiful is good: Evidence that the physically attractive are more socially skillful. *Journal of Experimental Social Psychology, 13,* 125-130.

Golla, F. L., & Hodge, S. R. (1949). Hormone treatment of the sexual offender. *The Lancet, 1,* 1006-1007.

Goode, W. J. (1959). The theoretical importance of love. *American Sociological Review, 24,* 38-47.

Goodman, R. H., Molitch, M. E., Post, K. D., & Jackson, I. M. D. (1980). Prolactin secreting adenomas in the male. In R. H. Goodman, M. E. Molitch, K. E. Post, & I. M. D. Jackson (Eds.), *The pituitary adenoma* (pp. 91-108). New York: Plenum Medical Book Press.

Goodwin, D. W. (1976). Psychiatric description and evaluation of the alcoholic. In R. E. Tarter & A. A. Sugerman (Eds.), *Alcoholism: Interdisciplinary approaches to an enduring problem* (pp. 203-223). Reading, MA: Addison-Wesley.

Gosden, R. G. (1985). *Biology of menopause. The causes and consequences of ovarian ageing.* Orlando, FL: Academic.

Gower, D. B., & Ruparelia, B. A. (1993). Olfaction in humans with special reference to odorous 16-androstenes: Their occurrence, perception and possible social, psychological and sexual impact. *Journal of Endocrinology, 137,* 167-187.

Graziano, W. G., Brothen, T., & Berscheid, E. (1978). Height and attraction: Do men and women see eye-to-eye? *Journal of Personality, 46,* 128-145.

Graziano, W. G., Jensen-Campbell, L. A., Todd, M., & Finch, J. F. (1997). Interpersonal attraction from an evolutionary psychology perspective: Women's reactions to dominant and prosocial men. In J. A. Simpson & D. T. Kenrick (Eds.), *Evolutionary social psychology* (pp. 141-167). Mahwah, NJ: Lawrence Erlbaum.

Green, S. E., & Mosher, D. L. (1985). A causal model of sexual arousal to erotic fantasies. *Journal of Sex Research, 21,* 1-23.

Greenblatt, R. B., McCall, E. F., & Torpin, R. (1941). Histologic changes in ovary following gonadotropin administration. *American Journal of Obstetrics and Gynecology, 42,* 983-996.

Greenblatt, R. B., Mortara, F., & Torpin, R. (1942). Sexual libido in the female. *American Journal of Obstetrics and Gynecology, 44,* 658-663.

Grinspoon, L., & Bakalar, J. B. (1981). Marihuana. In J. H. Lowinson & P. Ruiz (Eds.), *Substance abuse: Clinical problems and perspectives* (pp. 140-147). Baltimore, MD: Williams & Wilkins.

Halikas, J., Weller, R., & Morse, C. (1982). Effects of regular marijuana use on sexual performance. *Journal of Psychoactive Drugs, 14,* 59-70.

Hallstrom, T. (1979). Sexuality of women in middle age: The Goteborg study. *Journal of Biosocial Science Supplement, 6,* 165-175.

Hallstrom, T., & Samuelsson, S. (1990). Changes in women's sexual desire in middle life: The longitudinal study of women in Gothenburg. *Archives of Sexual Behavior, 19*, 259-268.

Halpern, C. T., Udry, J. R., Campbell, B., Suchindran, C., & Mason, G. A. (1994). Testosterone and religiosity as predictors of sexual attitudes and activity among adolescent males: A biosocial model. *Journal of Biosocial Science, 26*, 217-234.

Hames, C. T. (1980). Sexual needs and interests of postpartum couples. *Journal of Obstetric Gynecologic and Neonatal Nursing, 9*, 313-315.

Hamilton, M. (1980). Rating depressive patients. *Journal of Clinical Psychiatry, 41*, 21-24.

Hammerstein, J., Meckies, J., Leo-Rosberg, I., Moltz, L., & Zielske, F. (1975). Use of cyproterone acetate in the treatment of acne, hirsutism and virilism. *Journal of Steroid-Biochemistry, 6*, 827-836.

Hanbury, R., Cohen, M., & Stimmel, B. (1977). Adequacy of sexual performance in men maintained on methadone. *American Journal of Drug and Alcohol Abuse, 4*, 13-20.

Hart, R. D. (1960). Monthly rhythm of libido in married women. *British Medical Journal, 1*, 1023-1024.

Harvey, S. C. (1985). Hypnotics and sedatives. In A. G. Gilman, L. S. Goodman, T. W. Rall, & F. Murad (Eds.), *Goodman and Gilman's the pharmacological basis of therapeutics* (7th ed., pp. 339-371). New York: Macmillan.

Harvey, S. M. (1987). Female sexual behavior: Fluctuations during the menstrual cycle. *Journal of Psychosomatic Research, 31*, 101-110.

Harvey, S. M., & Beckman, L. J. (1986). Alcohol consumption, female sexual behavior and contraceptive use. *Journal of Studies on Alcohol, 47*, 327-332.

Hatfield, E. (1988). Passionate and companionate love. In R. J. Sternberg & M. L. Barnes (Eds.), *The psychology of love* (pp. 191-217). New Haven, CT: Yale University Press.

Hatfield, E., & Rapson, R. L. (1987). Passionate love/sexual desire: Can the same paradigm explain both? *Archives of Sexual Behavior, 16*, 259-278.

Hatfield, E., & Sprecher, S. (1986). Measuring passionate love in intimate relationships. *Journal of Adolescence, 9*, 383-410.

Hatfield, E., Traupmann, J., & Sprecher, S. (1984). Older women's perceptions of their intimate relationships. *Journal of Social and Clinical Psychology, 2*, 108-124.

Hatfield, E., & Walster, G. W. (1978). *A new look at love*. Reading, MA: Addison-Wesley.

Hazan, C., & Shaver, P. (1987). Romantic love conceptualized as an attachment process. *Journal of Personality and Social Psychology, 52*, 511-524.

Heider, F. (1958). *The psychology of interpersonal relations*. Hillsdale, NJ: Lawrence Erlbaum.

Heiman, J. R. (1975). Responses to erotica: An exploration of physiological and psychological correlates of human sexual response. *Dissertation Abstracts International, 36*(5-B), 2472.

Heiser, K., & Hartmann, U. (1987). Disorders of sexual desire in a sample of women alcoholics. *Drug and Alcohol Dependence, 19*, 145-157.

Heller, C. G., Laidlaw, W. M., Harvey, H. T., & Nelson, W. O. (1958). Effects of progestational compounds on the reproductive processes of the human male. *Annals of the New York Academy of Sciences, 71*, 649-665.

Hendrick, C., & Hendrick, S. (1986). A theory and method of love. *Journal of Personality and Social Psychology, 50*, 392-402.

Hendrick, C., Hendrick, S. S., & Dicke, A. (1998). The love attitudes scale: Short form. *Journal of Social and Personal Relationships, 15*, 147-159.

Hendrick, S., & Hendrick, C. (1992). *Liking, loving, & relating* (2nd ed.). Pacific Grove, CA: Brooks/Cole.

Herek, G. M., Kimmel, D. C., Amaro, H., & Melton, G. B. (1991). Avoiding heterosexist bias in psychological research. *American Psychologist, 9*, 957-963.

Herold, E. S., & Mewhinney, D. K. (1993). Gender differences in casual sex and AIDS prevention: A survey of dating bars. *Journal of Sex Research, 30*, 36-42.

Hill, E. M., Nocks, E. S., & Gardner, L. (1987). Physical attractiveness: Manipulation by physique and status displays. *Ethology and Sociobiology, 8*, 143-154.

Hofmann, A. D. (1983). Drug and alcohol use and abuse: Medical and psychologic aspects. In A. D. Hofmann & D. E. Greydanus (Eds.), *Adolescent medicine* (pp. 328-349). Menlo Park, CA: Addison-Wesley.

Hollister, L. E. (1975). The mystique of social drugs and sex. In M. Sandler & G. L. Gessa (Eds.), *Sexual behavior: Pharmacology and biochemistry* (pp. 85-92). New York: Raven.

Holt, E. B. (1931). *Animal drive and the learning process* (Vol. 1). New York: Henry Holt.

Holtzman, L. C. (1976). Sexual practices during pregnancy. *Journal of Nurse-Midwifery, 21*, 29-35.

Howell, J. R., Reynolds, C. F., III, Thase, M. E., Frank, E., Jennings, J. R., Houck, P. R., Berman, S., Jacobs, E., & Kupfer, D. J. (1987). Assessment of sexual function, interest and activity in depressed men. *Journal of Affective Disorders, 13*, 61-66.

Hucker, S., Langevin, R., & Bain, J. (1988). A double blind trial of sex drive reducing medication in pedophiles. *Annals of Sex Research, 1*, 227-242.

Huffer, V., Levin, L., & Aronson, H. (1970). Oral contraceptives: Depression and frigidity. *Journal of Nervous and Mental Disease, 151*, 35-41.

Hunter, R., & MacAlpine, I. (1963). *Three hundred years of psychiatry*. London: Oxford University Press.

Jackson, L. A., & Ervin, K. S. (1992). Height stereotypes of women and men: The liabilities of shortness for both sexes. *Journal of Social Psychology, 132*, 433-445.

Jaffe, J. H., & Martin, W. R. (1985). Opioid analgesics and antagonists. In A. G. Gilman, L. S. Goodman, T. W. Rall, & F. Murad (Eds.), *Goodman and Gilman's the pharmacological basis of therapeutics* (7th ed., pp. 491-531). New York: Macmillan.

James, W. (1950). *The principles of psychology* (Vol. 1). Dover. (Original work published 1890)

Jensen-Campbell, L. A., Graziano, W. G., & West, S. (1995). Dominance, prosocial orientation, and female preferences: Do nice guys really finish last? *Journal of Personality and Social Psychology, 68,* 427-440.

Jones, E. E., & McGillis, D. (1976). Correspondent inferences and the attribution cube: A comparative reappraisal. In J. H. Harvey, W. J. Ickes, & R. F. Kidd (Eds.), *New directions in attribution research* (Vol. 1, pp. 389-420). Hillsdale, NJ: Lawrence Erlbaum.

Julien, E., & Over, R. (1988). Male sexual arousal across five modes of erotic stimulation. *Archives of Sexual Behavior, 17,* 131-143.

Kalick, S. M. (1988). Physical attractiveness as a status cue. *Journal of Experimental Social Psychology, 24,* 469-489.

Kane, F. J., Lipton, M. A., & Ewing, J. A. (1969). Hormonal influences in female sexual response. *Archives of General Psychiatry, 20,* 202-209.

Kaplan, H. S. (1977). Hypoactive sexual desire. *Journal of Sex & Marital Therapy, 3,* 3-9.

Kaplan, H. S. (1979). *Disorders of sexual desire and other new concepts and techniques in sex therapy.* New York: Simon & Schuster.

Kaplan, H. S. (1992). A neglected issue: The sexual side effects of current treatments for breast cancer. *Journal of Sex & Marital Therapy, 18,* 3-19.

Kaplan, H. S., & Owett, T. (1993). The female androgen deficiency syndrome. *Journal of Sex & Marital Therapy, 19,* 3-24.

Karlson, P., & Lüscher, M. (1959). "Pheromones": A new term for a class of biologically active substances. *Nature, 183,* 55-56.

Kayner, C. E., & Zagar, J. A. (1983). Breast-feeding and sexual response. *Journal of Family Practice, 17,* 69-73.

Kazak, A. E., & Reppucci, N. D. (1980). Romantic love as a social institution. In K. S. Pope (Ed.), *On love and loving* (pp. 209-227). San Francisco, CA: Jossey-Bass.

Kennedy, B. J. (1973). Effect of massive doses of sex hormones on libido. *Medical Aspects of Human Sexuality, 7,* 67-78.

Kenny, J. A. (1973). Sexuality of pregnant and breastfeeding women. *Archives of Sexual Behavior, 2,* 215-229.

Kenrick, D. T. (1994). Evolutionary social psychology: From sexual selection to social cognition. *Advances in Experimental Social Psychology, 26,* 75-121.

Kenrick, D. T., Groth, G. E., Trost, M. R., & Sadalla, E. K. (1993). Integrating evolutionary and social exchange perspectives on relationships: Effects of gender, self-appraisal, and involvement level on mate selection criteria. *Journal of Personality and Social Psychology, 64,* 951-969.

Kenrick, D. T., Gutierres, S. E., & Goldberg, L. L. (1989). Influence of popular erotica on judgments of strangers and mates. *Journal of Experimental Social Psychology, 25,* 159-167.

Kenrick, D. T., Sadalla, E. K., Groth, G., & Trost, M. R. (1990). Evolution, traits, and the stages of human courtship: Qualifying the parental investment model. *Journal of Personality, 58,* 97-116.

Kephart, W. M. (1967). Some correlates of romantic love. *Journal of Marriage and the Family, 29,* 470-474.

Kinsey, A. C., Pomeroy, W. B., & Martin, C. E. (1948). *Sexual behavior in the human male.* Philadelphia, PA: W. B. Saunders.

Kinsey, A. C., Pomeroy, W. B., Martin, C. E., & Gebhard, P. H. (1953). *Sexual behavior in the human female.* Philadelphia, PA: W. B. Saunders.

Kirsch, I. (1990). *Changing expectations: A key to effective psychotherapy.* Pacific Grove, CA: Brooks/Cole.

Klassen, A. D., & Wilsnack, S. C. (1986). Sexual experience and drinking among women in a U.S. national survey. *Archives of Sexual Behavior, 15,* 363-392.

Koller, W. C., Vetere-Overfield, B., Williamson, A., Busenbark, K., Nash, J., & Parrish, D. (1990). Sexual dysfunction in Parkinson's disease. *Clinical Neuropharmacology, 13,* 461-463.

Koppelman, M. C. S., Parry, B. L., Hamilton, J. A., Alagna, S. W., & Loriaux, D. L. (1987). Effect of bromocriptine on mood, affect and libido in hyperprolactinemia. *American Journal of Psychiatry, 144,* 1037-1041.

Koster, A., & Garde, K. (1993). Sexual desire and menopausal development. A prospective study of Danish women born in 1936. *Maturitas, 16,* 49-60.

Krafft-Ebing, R. von (1945). *Psychopathia sexualis* (12th ed.). New York: Pioneer. (Original work published 1886)

Kramer, J. C. (1972). Introduction to amphetamine abuse. In E. H. Ellinwood & S. Cohen (Eds.), *Current concepts on amphetamine abuse* (pp. 177-184). Rockville, MD: National Institute of Mental Health.

Kravitz, H. M., Haywood, T. W., Kelly, J., Wahlstrom, C., Liles, S., & Cavanaugh, J. L. (1995). Medroxyprogesterone treatment for paraphiliacs. *Bulletin of the American Academy of Psychiatry and the Law, 23,* 19-33.

Kwan, M., Greenleaf, W. J., Mann, J., Crapo, L., & Davidson, J. M. (1983). The nature of androgen action on male sexuality: A combined laboratory-self-report study on hypogonadal men. *Journal of Clinical Endocrinology & Metabolism, 57,* 557-562.

Labrie, F., DuPont, A., Belanger, A., St. Arnaud, R., Giguere, M., Lacourciere, Y., Emond, J., & Monfette, G. (1986). Treatment of prostate cancer with gonadotropin-releasing hormone agonists. *Endocrine Reviews, 7,* 67-74.

Laessle, R. G., Tuschl, R. J., Schweiger, U., & Pirke, K. M. (1990). Mood changes and physical complaints during the normal menstrual cycle in healthy young women. *Psychoneuroendocrinology, 15,* 131-138.

Lamb, S. C., Jackson, L. A., Cassiday, P. B., & Priest, D. J. (1993). Body figure preferences of men and women: A comparison of two generations. *Sex Roles, 28,* 345-358.

Lavrakas, P. J. (1975). Female preferences for male physiques. *Journal of Research in Personality, 9,* 324-334.

Lee, J. A. (1973). *Colours of love.* Toronto: New Press.

Lee, J. A. (1988). Love-styles. In R. J. Sternberg & M. L. Barnes (Eds.), *The psychology of love* (pp. 38-67). New Haven, CT: Yale University Press.

Legros, J. J., Chiodera, P., & Servalis, J. (1980). Hormones and sexual impotence. In D. de Wied & P. A. van Keep (Eds.), *Hormones and the brain* (pp. 205-217). Lancaster, PA: MTP Press.

Leiblum, S., Bachmann, G., Kemmann, E., Colburn, D., & Schwartzman, L. (1983). Vaginal atrophy in the postmenopausal woman: The importance of sexual activity and hormones. *Journal of the American Medical Association, 249,* 2195-2198.

Leiblum, S. R., & Rosen, R. C. (1988). Introduction: Changing perspectives on sexual desire. In S. R. Leiblum & R. C. Rosen (Eds.), *Sexual desire disorders* (pp. 1-17). New York: Guilford.

Levine, S. B. (1982). A modern perspective on nymphomania. *Journal of Sex & Marital Therapy, 8,* 316-324.

Levine, S. B. (1984). An essay on the nature of sexual desire. *Journal of Sex & Marital Therapy, 10,* 83-96.

Levine, S. B. (1987). More on the nature of sexual desire. *Journal of Sex & Marital Therapy, 13,* 35-44.

Levy, J. A. (1994). Sex and sexuality in later life stages. In A. S. Rossi (Ed.), *Sexuality across the life course* (pp. 287-309). Chicago: University of Chicago Press.

Lewis, C. S. (1960). *The four loves.* London: Geoffrey Bles.

Lichtenberg, J. D. (1989). *Psychoanalysis and motivation.* New Jersey: The Analytic Press.

LoPiccolo, J., & Friedman, J. M. (1988). Broad spectrum treatment of low sexual desire: Integration of cognitive, behavioral and systemic therapy. In S. R. Leiblum & R. C. Rosen (Eds.), *Sexual desire disorders* (pp. 107-144). New York: Guilford.

Lumley, J. (1978). Sexual feelings in pregnancy and after childbirth. *Australian and New Zealand Journal of Obstetrics and Gynecology, 18,* 114-117.

Lunde, I., Larsen, G. K., Fog, E., & Garde, K. (1991). Sexual desire, orgasm, and sexual fantasies: A study of 625 Danish women born in 1910, 1936, and 1958. *Journal of Sex Education & Therapy, 17,* 111-115.

Macfarlane, A. J. (1975). Olfaction in the development of social preferences in the human neonate. *Ciba Foundation Symposia, 33,* 103-117.

Malamuth, N. M., Sockloskie, R. J., Koss, M. P., & Tanaka, J. S. (1991). Characteristics of aggressors against women: Testing a model using a national sample of college students. *Journal of Consulting and Clinical Psychology, 59,* 670-681.

Mansfield, P. K., Voda, A., & Koch, P. B. (1995). Predictors of sexual response changes in heterosexual midlife women. *Health Values, 19,* 10-20.

Maslow, A. H. (1987). *Motivation and personality* (3rd ed.). New York: Harper & Row.

Masters, W. H., & Johnson, V. E. (1966). *Human sexual response.* Boston, MA: Little, Brown.

Masters, W. H., Johnson, V. E., & Kolodny, R. C. (1982). *Human sexuality.* Boston, MA: Little, Brown and Company.

Masters, W. H., Johnson, V. E., & Kolodny, R. C. (1994). *Heterosexuality.* New York: HarperCollins.

Mathes, E. W. (1984). Convergence among measures of interpersonal attraction. *Motivation and Emotion, 8,* 77-84.

Mathew, R. J., & Weinman, M. L. (1982). Sexual dysfunctions in depression. *Archives of Sexual Behavior, 11,* 323-328.

Mathews, A., Whitehead, A., & Kellet, J. (1983). Psychological and hormonal factors in the treatment of female sexual dysfunction. *Psychological Medicine, 13,* 83-92.

Matteo, S., & Rissman, E. (1984). Increased sexual activity during the midcycle portion of the human menstrual cycle. *Hormones and Behavior, 18,* 249-255.

Mazenod, B., Pugeat, M., & Forest, M. G. (1988). Hormones, sexual function and erotic behavior in women. In J. M. A. Sitsen (Ed.), *Handbook of sexology: Vol. VI. The pharmacology and endocrinology of sexual function* (pp. 316-351). Amsterdam: Elsevier Science Publishers.

McCance, R. A., Luff, M. C., & Widdowson, E. E. (1937). Physical and emotional periodicity in women. *Journal of Hygiene, 37,* 571-611.

McCauley, E., & Ehrhardt, A. A. (1976). Female sexual response: Hormonal and behavioral interactions. *Primary Care, 3,* 455-476.

McCoy, N., & Davidson, J. M. (1985). A longitudinal study of the effects of menopause on sexuality. *Maturitas, 7,* 203-210.

McCullough, R. C. (1974). Rhythms of sexual desire and sexual activity in the human female. *Dissertation Abstracts International, 34,* 4669B-4670B.

Mehrabian, A. (1972). *Nonverbal communication.* Chicago: Aldine-Atherton.

Mendelson, J. H., & Mello, N. K. (1982). Hormones and psycho-sexual development in young men following chronic heroin use. *Neurobehavioral Toxicology and Teratology, 4,* 441-445.

Metts, S., Sprecher, S., & Regan, P. C. (1998). Communication and sexual desire. In P. A. Andersen & L. K. Guerrero (Eds.), *Handbook of communication and emotion: Research, theory, applications, and contexts* (pp. 353-377). Orlando, FL: Academic Press.

Meyers, S., & Berscheid, E. (1996). The language of love: The difference a preposition makes. *Personality and Social Psychology Bulletin, 23,* 347-362.

Mischel, W. (1966). A social-learning view of sex differences in behavior. In E. E. Maccoby (Ed.), *The development of sex differences* (pp. 56-81). Stanford, CA: Stanford University Press.

Mohl, B., & Pedersen, B. L. (1991). Men with inhibited sexual desire: The price of women's lib? *Nordisk Sexologi, 9,* 243-247.

Moll, A. (1933). *Libido sexualis.* New York: American Ethnological Press.

Money, J. (1970). Use of an androgen-depleting hormone in the treatment of male sex offenders. *Journal of Sex Research, 6,* 165-172.

Money, J., Leal, J., & Gonzalez-Heydrich, J. (1988). Aphrodisiology: History, folklore, efficacy. In J. M. A. Sitsen (Ed.), *Handbook of sexology: Vol. VI. The pharmacology and endocrinology of sexual function* (pp. 499-515). Amsterdam: Elsevier Science Publishers.

Monti-Bloch, L., & Grosser, B. I. (1991). Effect of putative pheromones on the electrical activity of the human vomeronasal organ and olfactory epithelium. *Journal of Steroid Biochemistry and Molecular Biology, 39,* 573-582.

Morgan, J. P. (1981). Amphetamine. In J. H. Lowinson & P. Ruiz (Eds.), *Substance abuse: Clinical problems and perspectives* (pp. 167-184). Baltimore, MD: Williams & Wilkins.

Mosher, D. L., & Abramson, P. R. (1977). Subjective sexual arousal to films of masturbation. *Journal of Consulting and Clinical Psychology, 45,* 796-807.

Mosher, D. L., Barton-Henry, M., & Green, S. E. (1988). Subjective sexual arousal and involvement: Development of multiple indicators. *Journal of Sex Research, 25,* 412-425.

Mosher, D. L., & White, B. B. (1980). Effects of committed or casual erotic guided imagery on females' subjective sexual arousal and emotional response. *Journal of Sex Research, 16,* 273-299.

Muller, P., Musch, K., & Wolf, A. S. (1979). Prolactin: Variables of personality and sexual behavior. In L. Zichella & P. Pancheri (Eds.), *Psychoneuroendocrinology in reproduction* (pp. 357-372). North Holland: Elsevier.

Mulligan, T., & Moss, C. R. (1991). Sexuality and aging in male veterans: A cross-sectional study of interest, ability, and activity. *Archives of Sexual Behavior, 20,* 17-25.

Murray, H. A., Barrett, W. G., Homburger, E., et al. (1938). *Explorations in personality.* New York: Oxford University Press.

Murstein, B. I. (1988). A taxonomy of love. In R. J. Sternberg & M. L. Barnes (Eds.), *The psychology of love* (pp. 13-37). New Haven, CT: Yale University Press.

Myers, L. S., & Morokoff, P. J. (1986). Physiological and subjective sexual arousal in pre- and postmenopausal women and postmenopausal women taking replacement therapy. *Psychophysiology, 23,* 283-292.

Naik, S., & Pennington, G. W. (1981). Female gonadal function: The ovary. In G. W. Pennington & S. Naik (Eds.), *Hormone analysis: Methodology and clinical interpretation* (Vol. 2, pp. 27-61). Boca Raton, FL: CRC Press.

Neubeck, G. (1972). The myriad motives for sex. *Sexual Behavior, 2,* 51-56.

Nevid, J. S. (1984). Sex differences in factors of romantic attraction. *Sex Roles,* *11,* 401-411.

Nicholson, B. (1984). Does kissing aid human bonding by semiochemical addiction? *British Journal of Dermatology, 111,* 623-627.

Nutter, D. E., & Condron, M. K. (1983). Sexual fantasy and activity patterns of females with inhibited sexual desire versus normal controls. *Journal of Sex & Marital Therapy, 9,* 276-282.

Nutter, D. E., & Condron, M. K. (1985). Sexual fantasy and activity patterns of males with inhibited sexual desire and males with erectile dysfunction versus normal controls. *Journal of Sex & Marital Therapy, 11,* 91-98.

O'Carroll, R., & Bancroft, J. (1984). Testosterone therapy for low sexual interest and erectile dysfunction in men: A controlled study. *British Journal of Psychiatry, 145,* 146-151.

O'Carroll, R., Shapiro, C., & Bancroft, J. (1985). Androgens, behaviour and nocturnal erection in hypogonadal men: The effects of varying the replacement dose. *Clinical Endocrinology, 23,* 527-538.

O'Sullivan, L. F., & Byers, E. S. (1992). College students' incorporation of initiator and restrictor roles in sexual dating interactions. *Journal of Sex Research, 29,* 435-446.

Pam, A., Plutchik, R., & Conte, H. R. (1975). Love: A psychometric approach. *Psychological Reports, 37,* 83-88.

Pennington, G. W., Naik, S., & Bevan, B. R. (1981). The pituitary gland. In G. W. Pennington & S. Naik (Eds.), *Hormone analysis: Methodology and clinical interpretation* (Vol. 1, pp. 119-156). Boca Raton, FL: CRC Press.

Perkins, R. P. (1979). Sexual behavior and response in relation to complications of pregnancy. *American Journal of Obstetrics and Gynecology, 134,* 498-505.

Persky, H., Dreisbach, L., Miller, W. R., O'Brien, C. P., Khan, M. A., Lief, H. I., Charney, N., & Strauss, D. (1982). The relation of plasma androgen levels to sexual behaviors and attitudes of women. *Psychosomatic Medicine, 44,* 305-319.

Pfeiffer, E., Verwoerdt, A., & Davis, G. C. (1972). Sexual behavior in middle life. *American Journal of Psychiatry, 128,* 82-1267.

Pietropinto, A. (1986). Inhibited sexual desire. *Medical Aspects of Human Sexuality, 20,* 46-49.

Przybyla, D. P. J., & Byrne, D. (1984). The mediating role of cognitive processes in self-reported sexual arousal. *Journal of Research in Personality, 18,* 54-63.

Purifoy, F. E., Grodsky, A., & Giambra, L. M. (1992). The relationship of sexual daydreaming to sexual activity, sexual drive, and sexual attitudes for women across the life span. *Archives of Sexual Behavior, 21,* 369-385.

Rabkin, J. G., Rabkin, R., & Wagner, G. (1995). Testosterone replacement therapy in HIV illness. *General Hospital Psychiatry, 17,* 37-42.

Reamy, K., White, S. E., Daniell, W. C., & Le Vine, E. S. (1982). Sexuality and pregnancy: A prospective study. *Journal of Reproductive Medicine, 27,* 321-327.

Regan, P. C. (1996a). Rhythms of desire: The association between menstrual cycle phases and female sexual desire. *Canadian Journal of Human Sexuality, 5*, 145-156.

Regan, P. C. (1996b). Sexual outcasts: The perceived impact of body weight on sexuality. *Journal of Applied Social Psychology, 26*, 1803-1815.

Regan, P. C. (1997). The impact of male sexual request style on perceptions of sexual interactions: The mediational role of beliefs about female sexual desire. *Basic and Applied Social Psychology, 19*, 519-532.

Regan, P. C. (1998a). Minimum mate selection standards as a function of perceived mate value, relationship context, and gender. *Journal of Psychology and Human Sexuality, 10*, 53-73.

Regan, P. C. (1998b). Of lust and love: Beliefs about the role of sexual desire in romantic relationships. *Personal Relationships, 5*, 139-157.

Regan, P. C. (1998c). What if you can't get what you want? Willingness to compromise ideal mate selection standards as a function of sex, mate value, and relationship context. *Personality and Social Psychology Bulletin, 24*, 1288-1297.

Regan, P. C. (in press). The role of sexual desire and sexual activity in dating relationships. *Social Behavior and Personality.*

Regan, P. C., & Berscheid, E. (1995). Gender differences in beliefs about the causes of male and female sexual desire. *Personal Relationships, 2*, 345-358.

Regan, P. C., & Berscheid, E. (1996). Beliefs about the state, goals, and objects of sexual desire. *Journal of Sex & Marital Therapy, 22*, 110-120.

Regan, P. C., & Berscheid, E. (1997). Gender differences in characteristics desired in a potential sexual and marriage partner. *Journal of Psychology and Human Sexuality, 9*, 25-37.

Regan, P. C., & Dreyer, C. S. (in press). Lust? Love? Status? Young adults' motives for engaging in casual sex. *Journal of Psychology and Human Sexuality, 11.*

Regan, P. C., Kocan, E. R., & Whitlock, T. (1998). Ain't love grand! A prototype analysis of romantic love. *Journal of Social and Personal Relationships, 15*, 411-420.

Regan, P. C., Levin, L., Sprecher, S., Cate, R., & Christopher, S. (1998). *Partner preferences: What characteristics do men and women desire in their short-term sexual and long-term romantic partners?*. Manuscript submitted for publication.

Regas, S. J., & Sprenkle, D. H. (1984). Functional family therapy and the treatment of inhibited sexual desire. *Journal of Marital and Family Therapy, 10*, 63-72.

Reik, T. (1944). *A psychologist looks at love.* New York: Farrar & Rinehart.

Reik, T. (1945). *Psychology of sex relations.* New York: Grove Press.

Reiss, I. L. (1960). *Premarital sexual standards in America.* New York: Free Press.

Reiss, I. L. (1967). *The social context of premarital sexual permissiveness.* New York: Holt, Rinehart, & Winston.

Reiss, I. L. (1981). Some observations on ideology and sexuality in America. *Journal of Marriage and the Family, 43,* 271-283.

Reiss, I. L. (1986a). *Journey into sexuality: An exploratory voyage.* New York: Prentice Hall.

Reiss, I. L. (1986b). A sociological journey into sexuality. *Journal of Marriage and the Family, 48,* 233-242.

‑idge, R. D., & Berscheid, E. (1989, May). *On loving and being in love: A necessary distinction.* Paper presented at the annual convention of the Midwestern Psychological Association, Chicago.

Riley, A. J. (1984). Prolactin and female sexual function. *British Journal of Sexual Medicine, 11,* 14-17.

Robson, K. M., Brant, H. A., & Kumar, R. (1981). Maternal sexuality during first pregnancy and after childbirth. *British Journal of Obstetrics and Gynaecology, 88,* 882-889.

Rosch, E. (1975). Cognitive representations of semantic categories. *Journal of Experimental Psychology, 104,* 192-233.

Rosch, E. (1978). Principles of categorization. In E. Rosch & B. B. Lloyd (Eds.), *Cognition and categorization* (pp. 27-48). Hillsdale, NJ: Lawrence Erlbaum.

Rousseau, L., DuPont, A., Labrie, F., & Couture, M. (1988). Sexuality changes in prostate cancer patients receiving antihormonal therapy combining the antiandrogen flutamide with medical (LHRH agonist) or surgical castration. *Archives of Sexual Behavior, 17,* 87-98.

Rowland, D. L., Heiman, J. R., Gladue, B. A., Hatch, J. P., Doering, C. H., & Weiler, S. J. (1987). Endocrine, psychological and genital response to sexual arousal in men. *Psychoneuroendocrinology, 12,* 149-158.

Rubin, R. T., Gouin, P. R., Lubin, A., Poland, R. E., & Pirke, K. M. (1976). Nocturnal increase of plasma testosterone in men: Relation to gonadotropins and prolactin. *Journal of Clinical Endocrinology and Metabolism, 40,* 1027-1033.

Rubin, Z. (1970). Measurement of romantic love. *Journal of Personality and Social Psychology, 16,* 265-273.

Rubin, Z. (1973). *Liking and loving: An invitation to social psychology.* New York: Holt, Rinehart, & Winston.

Ryding, E. (1984). Sexuality during and after pregnancy. *Acta Obstetricia et Gynecologica Scandinavica, 63,* 679-682.

Sadalla, E. K., Kenrick, D. T., & Vershure, B. (1987). Dominance and heterosexual attraction. *Journal of Personality and Social Psychology, 52,* 730-738.

Safir, M. P., & Almagor, M. (1991). Psychopathology associated with sexual dysfunction. *Journal of Clinical Psychology, 47,* 17-27.

Salmimies, P., Kockott, G., Pirke, K. M., Vogt, H. J., & Schill, W. B. (1982). Effects of testosterone replacement on sexual behavior in hypogonadal men. *Archives of Sexual Behavior, 11,* 345-353.

Salmon, U. J., & Geist, S. H. (1943). Effect of androgens upon libido in women. *Journal of Clinical Endocrinology, 3*, 235-238.

Salusso-Deonier, C. J., Markee, N. L., & Pedersen, E. L. (1993). Gender differences in the evaluation of physical attractiveness ideals for male and female body builds. *Perceptual and Motor Skills, 76*, 1155-1167.

Sanders, D., Warner, P., Backstrom, T., & Bancroft, J. (1983). Mood, sexuality, hormones and the menstrual cycle. I. Changes in mood and physical state: Description of subjects and method. *Psychosomatic Medicine, 45*, 487-501.

Schachter, S. (1964). The interaction of cognitive and physiological determinants of emotional state. In L. Berkowitz (Ed.), *Advances in experimental social psychology* (Vol. 1, pp. 49-80). New York: Academic Press.

Schiavi, R. C. (1990). Chronic alcoholism and male sexual dysfunction. *Journal of Sex & Marital Therapy, 16*, 23-33.

Schiavi, R. C., Schreiner-Engel, P., Mandeli, J., Schanzer, H., & Cohen, E. (1990). Healthy aging and male sexual function. *American Journal of Psychiatry, 147*, 766-771.

Schlenker, B. R. (1980). *Impression management: The self-concept, social identity, and interpersonal relations.* Malabar, FL: Robert E. Krieger.

Schover, L. R. (1986). Sexual dysfunction: When a partner complains of low sexual desire. *Medical Aspects of Human Sexuality, 20*, 8-116.

Schover, L. R., Evans, R. B., & von Eschenbach, A. C. (1987). Sexual rehabilitation in a cancer center: Diagnosis and outcome in 384 consultations. *Archives of Sexual Behavior, 16*, 445-461.

Schover, L. R., Novick, A. C., Steinmuller, D. R., & Goormastic, M. (1990). Sexuality, fertility, and renal transplantation: A survey of survivors. *Journal of Sex & Marital Therapy, 16*, 3-13.

Schreiner-Engel, P., & Schiavi, R. C. (1986). Lifetime psychopathology in individuals with low sexual desire. *Journal of Nervous and Mental Disease, 174*, 646-651.

Schreiner-Engel, P., Schiavi, R. C., Smith, J., & White, D. (1981). Sexual arousability and the menstrual cycle. *Psychosomatic Medicine, 43*, 199-214.

Schreiner-Engel, P., Schiavi, R. C., Vietorisz, D., Eichel, J. D. S., & Smith, H. (1985). Diabetes and female sexuality: A comparative study of women in relationships. *Journal of Sex & Marital Therapy, 11*, 165-175.

Schreiner-Engel, P., Schiavi, R. C., Vietorisz, D., & Smith, H. (1987). The differential impact of diabetes type on female sexuality. *Journal of Psychosomatic Research, 31*, 23-33.

Schreiner-Engel, P., Schiavi, R. C., White, D., & Ghizzani, A. (1989). Low sexual desire in women: The role of reproductive hormones. *Hormones and Behavior, 23*, 221-234.

Schwartz, M. F., Bauman, J. E., & Masters, W. H. (1982). Hyperprolactinemia and sexual disorders in men. *Biological Psychiatry, 17*, 861-876.

Segraves, K. B., & Segraves, R. T. (1991). Hypoactive sexual desire disorder: Prevalence and comorbidity in 906 subjects. *Journal of Sex & Marital Therapy, 17*, 55-58.

Shaver, P., Hazan, C., & Bradshaw, D. (1988). Love as attachment: The integration of three behavioral systems. In R. J. Sternberg & M. L. Barnes (Eds.), *The psychology of love* (pp. 68-99). New Haven, CT: Yale University Press.

Shaver, P. R., & Hazan, C. (1988). A biased overview of the study of love. *Journal of Social and Personal Relationships, 5*, 473-501.

Shepperd, J. A., & Strathman, A. J. (1989). Attractiveness and height: The role of stature in dating preference, frequency of dating, and perceptions of attractiveness. *Personality and Social Psychology Bulletin, 15*, 617-627.

Sherwin, B. B. (1985). Changes in sexual behavior as a function of plasma sex steroid levels in post-menopausal women. *Maturitas, 7*, 225-233.

Sherwin, B. B. (1988). A comparative analysis of the role of androgen in human male and female sexual behavior: Behavioral specificity, critical thresholds, and sensitivity. *Psychobiology, 16*, 416-425.

Sherwin, B. B., & Gelfand, M. M. (1987). The role of androgen in the maintenance of sexual functioning in oophorectomized women. *Psychosomatic Medicine, 49*, 397-409.

Sherwin, B. B., Gelfand, M. M., & Brender, W. (1985). Androgen enhances sexual motivation in females: A prospective, crossover study of sex steroid administration in the surgical menopause. *Psychosomatic Medicine, 47*, 339-351.

Shotland, R. L., & Craig, J. M. (1988). Can men and women differentiate between friendly and sexually interested behavior? *Social Psychology Quarterly, 51*, 66-73.

Silber, M. (1994). Menstrual cycle and work schedule: Effects on women's sexuality. *Archives of Sexual Behavior, 23*, 397-404.

Simon, W. (1974). The social, the erotic, and the sensual: The complexities of sexual scripts. In J. K. Cole & R. Deinstbier (Eds.), *The Nebraska symposium on motivation, 1973* (pp. 61-82). Lincoln: University of Nebraska Press.

Simon, W., & Gagnon, J. H. (1986). Sexual scripts: Permanence and change. *Archives of Sexual Behavior, 15*(2), 97-120.

Simpson, J. A., Campbell, B., & Berscheid, E. (1986). The association between romantic love and marriage: Kephart (1967) twice revisited. *Personality and Social Psychology Bulletin, 12*, 363-372.

Simpson, J. A., & Gangestad, S. W. (1991). Individual differences in sociosexuality: Evidence for convergent and discriminant validity. *Journal of Personality and Social Psychology, 60*, 870-883.

Singh, D. (1993). Adaptive significance of female physical attractiveness: Role of waist-to-hip ratio. *Journal of Personality and Social Psychology, 65*, 293-307.

Singh, D. (1995). Female judgment of male attractiveness and desirability for relationships: Role of waist-to-hip ratio and financial status. *Journal of Personality and Social Psychology, 69*, 1089-1101.

Singh, D., & Luis, S. (1995). Ethnic and gender consensus for the effect of waist-to-hip ratio on judgment of women's attractiveness. *Human Nature, 6*, 51-65.

Sitsen, J. M. A. (1988). Prescription drugs and sexual function. In J. M. A. Sitsen (Ed.), *Handbook of sexology: Vol. VI. The pharmacology and endocrinology of sexual function* (pp. 425-461). Amsterdam: Elsevier Science Publishers.

Skakkebaek, N. E., Bancroft, J., Davidson, D. W., & Warner, P. (1981). Androgen replacement with oral testosterone undecanoate in hypogonadal men: A double blind controlled study. *Clinical Endocrinology, 14*, 49-61.

Slob, A. K., van der Werff ten Bosch, J. J., van Hall, E. V., de Jong, F. H., Weijmar Schultz, W. C. M., & Eikelboom, F. A. (1993). Psychosexual functioning in women with complete testicular feminization: Is androgen replacement therapy preferable to estrogen? *Journal of Sex & Marital Therapy, 19*, 201-209.

Smith, D. E., Buxton, M. E., & Dammann, G. (1979). Amphetamine abuse and sexual dysfunction: Clinical and research considerations. In D. E. Smith, D. R. Wesson, M. E. Buxton, R. B. Seymour, J. T. Ungerleider, J. P. Morgan, A. J. Mandell, & G. Jara (Eds.), *Amphetamine use, misuse, and abuse: Proceedings of the national amphetamine conference, 1978* (pp. 228-248). Boston, MA: G. K. Hall.

Solberg, D. A., Butler, J., & Wagner, N. N. (1973). Sexual behavior in pregnancy. *New England Journal of Medicine, 288*, 1098-1103.

Spaulding, C. B. (1971). The romantic love complex in American culture. *Sociology and Social Research, 55*, 82-100.

Sprecher, S., & Regan, P. C. (1996). College virgins: How men and women perceive their sexual status. *Journal of Sex Research, 33*, 3-15.

Sprecher, S., & Regan, P. C. (1998). Passionate and companionate love in courting and young married couples. *Sociological Inquiry, 68*, 163-185.

Stanislaw, H., & Rice, F. J. (1988). Correlation between sexual desire and menstrual cycle characteristics. *Archives of Sexual Behavior, 17*, 499-508.

Stensaas, L. J., Lavker, R. M., Monti-Bloch, L., Grosser, B. I., & Berliner, D. L. (1991). Ultrastructure of the human vomeronasal organ. *Journal of Steroid Biochemistry and Molecular Biology, 39*, 553-560.

Sternberg, R. J. (1986). A triangular theory of love. *Psychological Review, 93*, 119-135.

Sternberg, R. J. (1988). Triangulating love. In R. J. Sternberg & M. L. Barnes (Eds.), *The psychology of love* (pp. 119-138). New Haven, CT: Yale University Press.

Sternberg, R. J., & Barnes, M. L. (Eds.). (1988). *The psychology of love.* New Haven, CT: Yale University Press.

Stewart, D. E. (1989). Positive changes in the premenstrual period. *Acta Psychiatrica Scandinavia, 79*, 400-405.

Stuart, F. M., Hammond, D. C., & Pett, M. A. (1986). Psychological characteristics of women with inhibited sexual desire. *Journal of Sex & Marital Therapy, 12*, 108-115.

Stuart, F. M., Hammond, D. C., & Pett, M. A. (1987). Inhibited sexual desire in women. *Archives of Sexual Behavior, 16,* 91-106.

Studd, J. W. W., Collins, W. P., Chakravarti, S., Newton, J. R., Oram, D., & Parsons, A. (1977). Oestradiol and testosterone implants in the treatment of psychosexual problems in the postmenopausal woman. *British Journal of Obstetrics & Gynaecology, 84,* 314-315.

Suman, H. C. (1990). The role of physical attractiveness and eye-contact in sexual attraction. *Journal of Personality and Clinical Studies, 6,* 109-112.

Surra, C. A. (1990). Research and theory on mate selection and premarital relationships in the 1980s. *Journal of Marriage and the Family, 52,* 844-865.

Swensen, C. H. (1961). Love: A self-report analysis with college students. *Journal of Individual Psychology, 17,* 167-171.

Swensen, C. H., & Gilner, F. (1963). Factor analysis of self-report statements of love relationships. *Journal of Individual Psychology, 19,* 186-188.

Symmers, W. St. C. (1968). Carcinoma of the breast in transsexual individuals after surgical and hormonal interference with primary and secondary sex characteristics. *British Medical Journal, 2,* 83-85.

Talmadge, L. D., & Talmadge, W. C. (1986). Relational sexuality: An understanding of low sexual desire. *Journal of Sex & Marital Therapy, 12,* 3-21.

Tennent, G., Bancroft, J., & Cass, J. (1974). The control of deviant sexual behavior by drugs: A double-blind controlled study of benperidol, chlorpromazine, and placebo. *Archives of Sexual Behavior, 3,* 261-271.

Tennov, D. (1979). *Love and limerence.* New York: Stein & Day.

Thase, M. E., Reynolds, C. F., Jennings, J. R., Frank, E., Howell, J. R., Houck, P. R., Berman, S., & Kupfer, D. J. (1988). Nocturnal penile tumescence is diminished in depressed men. *Biological Psychiatry, 24,* 33-46.

Tinklepaugh, O. L. (1933). The nature of periods of sex desire in women and their relation to ovulation. *American Journal of Obstetrics and Gynecology, 26,* 335-345.

Tolman, E. C. (1932). *Purposive behavior in animals and men.* New York: Century.

Tolor, A., & DiGrazia, P. V. (1976). Sexual attitudes and behavior patterns during and following pregnancy. *Archives of Sexual Behavior, 5,* 539-551.

Townsend, J. M., & Levy, G. D. (1990). Effects of potential partners' physical attractiveness and socioeconomic status on sexuality and partner selection. *Archives of Sexual Behavior, 19,* 149-164.

Trivers, R. L. (1972). Parental investment and sexual selection. In B. Campbell (Ed.), *Sexual selection and the descent of man* (pp. 136-179). Chicago: Aldine.

Troland, L. T. (1928). *The fundamentals of human motivation.* New York: Van Nostrand.

Trudel, G. (1991). Review of psychological factors in low sexual desire. *Sexual and Marital Therapy, 6,* 261-272.

Udry, J. R., Billy, J. O. G., Morris, N. M., Groff, T. R., & Raj, M. H. (1985). Serum androgenic hormones motivate sexual behavior in adolescent boys. *Fertility and Sterility, 43,* 90-94.

Udry, J. R., & Morris, N. M. (1977). The distribution of events in the human menstrual cycle. *Journal of Reproduction and Fertility, 51*, 419-425.

Ungerleider, J. T., & De Angelis, G. G. (1981). Hallucinogens. In J. H. Lowinson & P. Ruiz (Eds.), *Substance abuse: Clinical problems and perspectives* (pp. 148-157). Baltimore, MD: Williams & Wilkins.

Useche, B., Villegas, M., & Alzate, H. (1990). Sexual behavior of Colombian high school students. *Adolescence, 25*, 291-304.

Van Dyke, C. (1981). Cocaine. In J. H. Lowinson & P. Ruiz (Eds.), *Substance abuse: Clinical problems and perspectives* (pp. 158-166). Baltimore, MD: Williams & Wilkins.

Van Thiel, D. H., Gavaler, J. S., & Tarter, R. E. (1988). The effects of alcohol on sexual behavior and function. In J. M. A. Sitsen (Ed.), *Handbook of sexology: Vol. VI. The pharmacology and endocrinology of sexual function* (pp. 478-498). Amsterdam: Elsevier Science Publishers.

Vandereycken, W. (1987). On desire, excitement, and impotence in modern sex therapy. *Psychotherapy and Psychosomatics, 47*, 175-180.

Verhulst, J., & Heiman, J. R. (1979). An interactional approach to sexual dysfunctions. *American Journal of Family Therapy, 7*, 19-36.

Walker, A., & Bancroft, J. (1990). Relationship between premenstrual symptoms and oral contraceptive use: A controlled study. *Psychosomatic Medicine, 52*, 86-96.

Wallace, P. (1977). Individual discrimination of humans by odor. *Physiology & Behavior, 19*, 577-579.

Wallen, K. (1990). Desire and ability: Hormones and the regulation of female sexual behavior. *Neuroscience & Biobehavioral Reviews, 14*, 233-241.

Walster, E., Aronson, V., Abrahams, D., & Rottman, L. (1966). Importance of physical attractiveness in dating behavior. *Journal of Personality and Social Psychology, 4*, 508-516.

Walster, E., & Berscheid, E. (1971). Adrenaline makes the heart grow fonder. *Psychology Today, 5*, 47-62.

Warner, P., & Bancroft, J. (1988). Mood, sexuality, oral contraceptives and the menstrual cycle. *Journal of Psychosomatic Research, 32*, 417-427.

Washton, A. M., Gold, M. S., & Pottash, A. C. (1984). Upper-income cocaine abusers. In *Advances in alcohol & substance abuse: Vol 4. Alcohol and drug abuse in the affluent* (pp. 51-57). New York: Haworth.

Waterman, G. S., Dahl, R. E., Birmaher, B., Ambrosini, P., Rabinovich, H., Williamson, D., Novacenko, H., Nelson, B., Puig-Antich, J., & Ryan, N. D. (1994). The 24-hour pattern of prolactin secretion in depressed and normal adolescents. *Biological Psychiatry, 35*, 440-445.

Waxenberg, S. E., Drellich, M. G., & Sutherland, A. M. (1959). The role of hormones in human behavior: I. Changes in female sexuality after adrenalectomy. *Journal of Clinical Endocrinology, 19*, 193-202.

Waxenberg, S. E., Finkbeiner, J. A., Drellich, M. G., & Sutherland, A. M. (1960). The role of hormones in human behavior. *Psychosomatic Medicine, 12*, 435-442.

Wedeck, H. E. (1961). *Dictionary of aphrodisiacs.* New York: Philosophical Library.

Weil, A. T. (1976). Letters from Andrew Weil: The love drug. *Journal of Psychedelic Drugs, 8,* 335-337.

Weizman, R., Weizman, A., Levi, J., Gura, V., Zevin, D., Maoz, B., Wijsenbeek, H., & David, M. B. (1983). Sexual dysfunction associated with hyperprolactinemia in males and females undergoing hemodialysis. *Psychosomatic Medicine, 45,* 259-269.

Wesson, D. R., & Smith, D. E. (1981). Abuse of sedative-hypnotics. In J. H. Lowinson & P. Ruiz (Eds.), *Substance abuse: Clinical problems and perspectives* (pp. 185-190). Baltimore, MD: Williams & Wilkins.

White, G. L., Fishbein, S., & Rutstein, J. (1981). Passionate love and the misattribution of arousal. *Journal of Personality and Social Psychology, 41,* 56-62.

Whittaker, L. H. (1959). Oestrogens and psychosexual disorders. *Medical Journal of Australia, 2,* 547-554.

Wiggins, J. S., Wiggins, N., & Conger, J. C. (1968). Correlates of heterosexual somatic preference. *Journal of Personality and Social Psychology, 10,* 82-90.

Wikler, A. (1952). A psychodynamic study of a patient during experimental self-regulated re-addiction to morphine. *Psychiatry Quarterly, 26,* 270-293.

Wilson, G. D. (1988). Measurement of sex fantasy. *Sexual and Marital Therapy, 3,* 45-55.

Wilson, T. D., & Klaaren, K. J. (1992). "Expectation whirls me round:" The role of affective expectations in affective experience. In M. S. Clark (Ed.), *Review of personality and social psychology: Vol. 14. Emotion and social behavior* (pp. 1-31). Newbury Park, CA: Sage.

Wilson, T. D., Lisle, D. J., Kraft, D., & Wetzel, C. G. (1989). Preferences as expectation-driven inferences: Effects of affective expectations on affective experience. *Journal of Personality and Social Psychology, 56,* 519-530.

Winick, C. (1981). Substances of abuse and sexual behavior. In J. H. Lowinson & P. Ruiz (Eds.), *Substance abuse: Clinical problems and perspectives* (pp. 582-590). Baltimore, MD: Williams & Wilkins.

Woodruff, R. A., Murphy, G. E., & Herjanic, M. (1967). The natural history of affective disorders. I. Symptoms of 72 patients at the time of index hospitalization admission. *Journal of Psychiatric Research, 5,* 255-263.

Wright, R. (1994). *The moral animal: The new science of evolutionary psychology.* New York: Pantheon.

Young, C. R. (1987). Antiandrogenic treatment in a university setting. *Journal of American College Health, 35,* 277-278.

Young, R. C., Schreiber, M. T., & Nysewander, R. W. (1983). Psychotic mania. *Biological Psychiatry, 18,* 1167-1173.

Youngstrom, N. (1991). Sex behavior studies are derailed. *APA Monitor, 22,* 1, 29.

Zellman, G. L., & Goodchilds, J. D. (1983). Becoming sexual in adolescence. In E. A. Allgeier & N. B. McCormick (Eds.), *Changing boundaries: Gender roles and sexual behavior* (pp. 49-63). Palo Alto, CA: Mayfield.

Index

Affective expectations, sexual desire
    and, 70
Age:
    stereotypes about, 32, 55, 56
    hormonal changes and, 51, 55
    sexual desire and, 55-56
Alcohol, sexual desire and, 60-61
Amphetamine, sexual desire and, 62-63
Androgens:
    exogenous, 36-37
    minimum amounts of, 38
    replacement therapy and, 36
    sexual desire and, 34-39
    synthesis of, 34
Antiandrogens, sexual desire and, 35-36
Aphrodisiac, 59, 110
Attachment, 122

Barbiturates, sexual desire and, 61

Climacteric, 50

Cocaine, sexual desire and, 63
Colors of love. *See* Love styles
Companionate love, 119, 127-128, 132,
    133
Coolidge effect. *See* Novelty
Cyproterone acetate. *See* Antiandrogens

Depressants:
    physiological and psychological
        effects of, 60
    sexual desire and, 60-62
Depression, sexual desire and. *See* Mood
Desire, general state of, 13-15

Emotional state, sexual desire and,
    83-86, 108
Erotic love. *See* Romantic love; Love
    styles
Erotophobia-erotophilia, sexual desire
    and, 80
Estradiol. *See* Estrogens

Estrogens:
    exogenous, administration of, 41
    gynecological problems and, 41
    sexual desire and, 40-41
    synthesis of, 39
Estrone. See Estrogens
Evolutionary theory:
    romantic love and, 122-123
    sexual desirability and, 90-91
Eye contact, sexual attraction and,
    101-102

Freudian theory. See Psychoanalytic
    theory

Gender differences:
    amount of sexual desire and, 58
    beliefs about sexual desire and, 75
    knowledge about sexual desire
        and, 77-78
    sexual desire disorders and, 57-58
    willingness to report sexual desire
        and, 58-59

Hallucinogens:
    physiological and psychological
        effects of, 65
    sexual desire and, 65
Health. See Physical health
Height, sexual desirability and, 95-96
Heroin, sexual desire and, 64
Homosexuality:
    early views of, 3-4
    romantic love and, 111, 118, 135-136
Hormonally mediated life events, sexual
    desire and, 46-52
Hormones, sexual desire and, 7, 34-46
Hyperprolactinemia. See Prolactin
Hypoactive sexual desire disorder. See
    Inhibited sexual desire

Inhibited sexual desire, 38-39, 57, 72,
    80-81, 108

Lactation, sexual desire and, 44
Libido, 4
Limerence, 120
Love. See Romantic love
Love styles, 120

Marijuana:
    physiological and psychological
        effects of, 65-66
    sexual desire and, 66
Masturbation, 2
Medroxyprogesterone acetate. See
    Antiandrogens
Menopause:
    definition of, 50-51
    hormonal events during, 51
    physiological events during, 51
    sexual desire and, 51-52
Menstrual cycle:
    hormones involved in, 46-47
    length of, 46
    measurement of, 46-47
    sexual desire and, 46-50
Methadone, sexual desire and, 64-65
Methaqualone, sexual desire and, 61-62
Mood, sexual desire and, 82-83
Morphine, sexual desire and, 63-64

Novelty:
    romantic love and, 119
    sexual desire and, 102-104

Opiates:
    physiological and psychological
        effects of, 63
    sexual desire and, 63-65
Opium, sexual desire and, 63-4
Ovulation:
    sexual desire and, 46-47
    timing of, 46

Passionate love. See Romantic love
Passionate Love Scale, 125-126, 128
Perimenopause, 50
Personality, sexual desire and, 79-81

Pheromones, sexual desire and, 7, 104-106
Physical attractiveness, sexual desirability and, 91, 93-95
Physical health, sexual desire and, 53-54
Physiological arousal, sexual desire and. *See* Emotional state
Physique, sexual desirability and, 95-96
Physique display, sexual desirability and, 97-98
Pornography, impact on sexual desire, 106-107
Pregnancy:
  hormonal changes during, 50
  sexual desire and, 50
Progesterone:
  oral contraceptives containing, 42-43
  sexual desire and, 42-43
  synthesis of, 42
Prolactin:
  androgen production and, 45
  excessive amounts of, 43
  lactation and, 43-44
  mood and, 45
  sexual behavior and, 43
  sexual desire and, 43-45
  synthesis of, 43
Prototype approach, 130
Psychoanalytic theory, 4, 112
Puberty. *See* Age

Rape myths, 73
Recreational drug use:
  disinhibition and, 67
  psychological expectations and, 67-68
  sexual desire and, 59-67
Relationship quality, sexual desire and, 107-109, 139-140
Rhythm method of contraception, 47
Romantic love:
  as a cause of sexual desire, 110, 138-139
  as a heterosexual experience, 111, 118, 135-136
  as limerence, 120

as a mixture of affection and sexual desire, 111-112, 114, 115, 121
as an asexual experience, 116-118
as interpersonal attraction, 116-117
as the sublimation of sexual desire, 112
as thwarted sexual desire, 113
association between sexuality and, 119-124
evolutionary significance of, 122-123
importance of, 116
measures of, 117, 123, 125-126
mislabeled as sexual desire, 73
physiological arousal and, 119
prototype of, 130-131
sexual desire and, 111-116, 124-136
sexual excitement and, 127

Sex appeal. *See* Sexual desirability
Sex differences, sexual desire and. *See* Gender differences
Sex research, 2-9
  comparative (animal) studies, 6-7
  focus on pathology, 2-3
  focus on normal sexual function, 3-4
  Kinsey, 5-6
  Masters and Johnson, 8-9
Sexual activity, 18-20
  distinguished from sexual desire, 18-19
Sexual arousal, 8, 10, 15-18
  distinguished from sexual desire, 17-18
  physiological-genital, 15-16
  subjective, 16-17
Sexual customs. *See* Sexual scripts
Sexual desirability:
  beliefs about, 91-93
  height and, 95
  nonverbal behavior and, 101-102
  novelty and, 102-103
  pheromones and, 104-106
  physical attractiveness and, 93-95
  physique and, 95-97
  physique display and, 97-98
  pornography and, 106-107
  social status and, 91, 98-101

theories about, 89-91
  waist-to-hip ratio and, 96
  weight and, 96-97
Sexual desire:
  adaptive function of, 10
  beliefs about, 32-33, 74-79
  consequences of, 138-139
  definition of, 15
  dimensions of, 20-21
  integrative model of, 28-30
  love and, 76-78
  measurement of, 30-31, 33
  misinterpretation of, 73, 115
  motivational views of, 22-28
  relational views of, 28
Sexual excitement. See Sexual arousal
Sexual fantasy, 30
Sexual response cycle:
  in animals, 7-8
  in humans, 8-9
  inclusion of sexual desire in, 10
  co-occurrence of events in, 20
Sexual scripts, sexual desire and, 71

Sexual standards, 72-73
Sexual trauma, sexual desire and, 81
Social role theory, sexual desirability
  and, 89-90
Social status, sexual desirability and, 91,
  98-101
Sociocultural norms, sexual desire and,
  70-72, 89
Stimulants:
  physiological and psychological
    effects of, 62
  sexual desire and, 62-63

Testosterone. See Androgens
Touch, sexual attraction and, 101-102
Triangular Theory of Love, 121

Waist-to-hip ratio, sexual desirability
  and, 96
Weight, sexual desirability and, 96-97

About the Authors

Pamela C. Regan is Associate Professor of Psychology at California State University, Los Angeles. She received her Ph.D. in psychology from the University of Minnesota. Her research interests are in the areas of close relationships and human sexuality, with an emphasis on passionate love, sexual desire, and mate preference. She directs the Social Relations Lab at CSU Los Angeles and has published numerous journal articles, book chapters, and reviews on sex, love, and mating.

Ellen Bersheid is Professor of Psychology at the University of Minnesota. She received her degree in psychology from the University of Minnesota. Her research interests are in the areas of close relationships, interpersonal attraction, and emotion. In 1998, she was honored by the American Psychological Association and by the International Society for the Study of Personal Relationships for her outstanding contributions to the field of psychology and to the science of close relationships.